FRANCIS OF ASSISI
The Message in His Writings

Thaddée Matura OFM

Translated by
Paul Barrett, OFMCap

FRANCIS OF ASSISI
The Message in His Writings

Thaddée Matura OFM

Translated by
Paul Barrett OFMCap

Franciscan Institute Publications
St. Bonaventure University
St. Bonaventure, New York 14778

1997

This is a translation of *François d'Assise, "Auteur Spirituel": Le message de ses écrits* by Thaddée Matura OFM, *Les Éditions du Cerf*, 29 boulevard Latour-Maubourg, 75340 Paris Cedex 07, France, 1996.

Translator's Note:

The best available English translation of Francis's writings is to be found in Regis J. Armstrong and Ignatius C. Brady's *Francis and Clare: the Complete Works* (Mahwah, NJ: Paulist Press, 1982), which was used in preparing this translation. Armstrong-Brady differ slightly from Matura in their listing of Francis's writings. For example, Matura lists only one *Letter to the Custodians*, while Armstrong-Brady give two; Matura lists the Marian Antiphon from the *Office of the Passion* separately, while Armstrong-Brady include it in the *Office*; Matura lists only three of the seven "Dictated Writings" given by Armstrong-Brady, but the other four are quite short, averaging only about four lines each. These differences are unimportant for the purposes of this book.

ISBN 1-57659-127-1

Printed at
   BookMasters, Inc.
   Mansfield, Ohio

CONTENTS

Contents

Abbreviations

Adm	Admonitions
AntOffPass	Antiphon in Office of the Passion
BenBer	Blessing for Brother Bernard
BenLeo	Blessing for Brother Leo*
CantExh	Canticle of Exhortation for St. Clare and Her Sisters
CantSol	Canticle of Brother Sun
EpAnt	Letter to St. Anthony
EpCler	Letter to the Clergy
1EpCust	First Letter to the Custodians
2EpCust	Second Letter to the Custodians
1EpFid	First Version of the Letter to the Faithful
2EpFid	Second Version of the Letter to the Faithful
EpLeo	Letter to Brother Leo
EpMin	Letter to a Minister
EpOrd	Letter to the Entire Order
EpRect	Letter to the Rulers of the Peoples
ExhLd	Exhortation to the Praise of God
ExpPat	Prayer Inspired by the Our Father
FormViv	Form of Life Given to St. Clare and Her Sisters
LaudDei	Praises of God*
LaudHor	Praises to be Said at All the Hours
OffPass	Office of the Passion
OrCruc	Prayer Before the Crucifix
RegB	Later Rule (1223)
RegErm	Rule for Hermitages
RegNB	Earlier Rule (1221)
SalBMV	Salutation of the Blessed Virgin Mary
SalVirt	Salutation of the Virtues
Test	Testament
TestSen	Testament of Siena
UltVol	Last Will Written for St. Clare
VPLaet	True and Perfect Joy

*__BenLeo__ and **LaudDei** are to be found under "The Parchment Given to Brother Leo" in Armstrong-Brady: *Francis and Clare: the Complete Works*, pp.99f.

Foreword

I have always felt drawn more to Francis's own writings than to the various biographies of the Saint that have appeared over the centuries, perhaps because the medieval lives are written in the bombastic, turgid style of the thirteenth century, while the modern ones tend to be repetitive and overly dramatic. The purpose of both these types of biography is to depict Francis as a heroic figure; that is, they are principally concerned with the "cult of personality." The Saint's writings, however, have been so eclipsed by highly colored accounts of what he said and did that they are generally regarded as poor relations, barely acknowledged as his.

Yet, strangely enough, it was these writings that most attracted me, even though, at the time, they were little known and less read. From the beginning of my life as a Franciscan, I was fascinated by the lyrical nature of the writings, their quasi-liturgical style, and their aura of mysticism. I remember copying out the simple yet majestic Latin text of the passages that struck me, such as the *Praises of God* and the imposing chapter twenty-three of the *Earlier Rule*.

Later, during my biblical studies, I found that Francis's arrangement of the Psalms showed an insight into Scripture and its use in the liturgy that was closer to the patristic period than to the Middle Ages, in which he lived. For some thirty years now, I have been reading the writings closely and applying to them the principles of biblical interpretation, both out of personal interest as well as for use in my work in the formation of youth. During that time, I have been able to examine and place in context each of the writings, analyzing the structure and contents of the various texts and attempting to form a synthesis of particular themes. I have used the results of these studies as material for lectures, courses, and articles in various publications.

I have gradually become convinced that the message conveyed in Francis's writings and the one which all the biographical literature attributes to him, not only do not overlap, but positively diverge, if only because the focus of each is different.

This present study aims at being more than just a detailed introduction to each of the writings and more than a mere detailing of the particular themes that run through them. I realize that, in recent years, this work has already been done from various perspectives. But we have not yet had a systematic analysis of the global vision that inspired Francis to write. We still cannot answer the question: what view of God or humanity or human conduct is to be found on or just below the surface of these texts? That is the problem I am trying to solve here.

I am aware of the difficulties and limitations of this enterprise. As an exegete, an interpreter of Scripture, accustomed to analyzing texts carefully, I know that making a synthesis is dangerous and full of pitfalls. On the one hand, such a venture demands simplification, abbreviation, summarizing and consequently the loss of much of the richness and many of the nuances of the text. And on the other hand, a synthesis presupposes a unifying center to give it coherence and balance, a center that must be derived from the texts themselves and not imposed from outside. Moreover, in any body of writings which were occasioned by particular circumstances, such a center is not immediately apparent.

In addition, we must ask ourselves if this study should be highly technical and therefore of interest only to some specialists, or should it be, instead, so popular and so accessible to everyone that it runs the risk of being regarded as superficial. We have tried to keep a foot in both camps by using two approaches, sometimes employing meticulous, even perhaps tedious, analysis, and at other times expressing opinions that may seem completely subjective and groundless. We shall often have occasion to deal with the same texts and themes more than once but from different angles, and this may seem repetitive. However, if readers are bored or put off by this, we beg them to be patient and wait until they reach the end of the book before making a final judgment. They should also be aware that our synthesis is not meant to be the last word but only a rough sketch and an invitation to investigate further.

As we have already said, only too many of Francis's biographies indulged in the "cult of personality" and presented him as "the greatest of all the saints." We do not wish to fall into the same trap by trying to show that the Saint's message in his writings was "the greatest and most exalted spirituality" ever taught, even though we are fully convinced of its depth, balance, and relevance today—features which, we hasten to add, are also shared by the teaching of the other schools of spirituality!

Of set purpose, we have not dissected Francis's message and applied it to present-day situations. That is not necessary because the message is still there to be read, even if one must sometimes read between the lines. Here we have simply tried to provide material for further study by bringing together the main elements of his thought, and we leave to the reader and the critic the task of interpreting the Saint's lessons for today.

Part One, the introduction to Francis and his message, is divided into two chapters. In the first chapter, we distinguish between Francis, the historical figure, and his written message; and we then consider the form, contents, context, and sources of each of the pieces, some thirty in number, which contain the message, as well as the studies and commentaries on it.

In chapter 2, we comment on two of the major texts, namely, chapter 23 of the *Earlier Rule* (RegNB) and the *Second Letter to the Faithful* (2EpFid), to provide a key to reading and interpreting the writings as a whole.

In Part Two, the longest section of the book, we deal with those parts of the message which refer to God and to humanity as inseparable from each other and as considered from the historical and dynamic points of view. We study, first, the primacy of the Father in the community of the Trinity (chapter 1). Next, we examine the two aspects of our humanity, our greatness and our wretchedness, both as individuals and as a community (chapter 2). Finally, we describe the journey of conversion (chapter 3) and the different vocations which Francis distinguished and suggested (chapter 4).

Part Three is the shortest in the book, and, by way of conclusion, it summarizes the results of our study and leaves them open for interpretation.

We can only hope that our analyses, syntheses, and commentaries will serve to enkindle in the readers' hearts some of the fire that burns in Francis's words and will help them towards a better understanding and a greater love of "the words of our Lord Jesus Christ, who is the Word of the Father, and the words of the Holy Spirit, which are spirit and life" (2EpFid 3).

Practical Advice

As the subtitle indicates, the object of this study is the message conveyed by Francis's writings, which, while they are frequently quoted and commented upon, are not normally given here in full. Those readers who are familiar with Francis's texts will find their way without difficulty through our analyses and explanations. However, others may wish to read the writings before continuing with the rest of this book or simply keep them at hand for reference as the occasion arises.

While we have consulted almost everything that has been published on the various points raised in the book, we have decided not to burden the text with the learned apparatus of footnotes and references. Instead, we have supplied a bibliography which should be of use to those who wish to pursue further studies on Francis's writings

Part I

The Message and the Medium

Chapter 1

The Man and His Message

Francis of Assisi (1182-1226) is one of the most thoroughly documented figures in history and, in our ecologically-conscious age, he is one of the best known and perhaps even the most popular of all. His first biography, Thomas of Celano's *First Life of St. Francis*, was written scarcely two years after his death. From then on, he has continued to be written and spoken about almost unceasingly. In fact, in modern times, several new biographies of the Saint in different languages are published almost every year. And who today does not know about and is even able to quote from his prayer for peace, apocryphal though it may be? Yet, apart from his prayer for peace and perhaps some phrases from his *Canticle of Brother Sun*, the general public knows little or nothing about his writings. But they do know about Francis as a figure in history and about the events of his short life of forty-four years as recorded in the medieval and modern biographies. In the forty years after Francis's death, there appeared several biographies whose authors we know, namely, the two lives by Thomas of Celano, which came out in 1228 and 1248, and the two versions of the life by St. Bonaventure in 1262. During the same period, there appeared several anonymous lives, of uncertain dates and under different titles, such as the *Anonymous of Perugia*, the *Legend of the Three Companions*, the *Legend of Perugia* (also called the *Compilation of Assisi*) and, later, the *Mirror of Perfection*.

This considerable body of material was focused on Francis, since medieval biographies were really hagiographies, that is, writings about people who were regarded as holy (*hagios*). So, the subject of such a biography was always seen as a heroic figure, whose life, words, virtues, and miracles were described in loving detail. Of course, we acknowledge fully the deep impression that Francis's personality made on his contemporaries, especially those closest to him, and we do not cast any doubt upon or wish to minimize the solid historical foundation for these accounts. But like any testimony, these first biographies are marked by the cultural and religious upbringing and outlook of those who provided them, by the atmosphere and ideals of the times, and by the writers' personal choice of material and the way they viewed and understood the person whom they were describing.

The aim of a biography is to describe someone and, in the case of a saint, to extol him/her and hold him/her up as a model for others to imitate. The subject's human and spiritual traits of character and his/her words and deeds form the message the writer wishes to convey to the reader. As a consequence, the *man/woman* becomes identified with the *message*: so that it is the *image*, and not the person, that speaks. Often no consideration is given to the fact that the person concerned—in this case, Francis—may have left a body of writings and therefore a specific message that cannot be conveyed by a biography which can easily be little more than a surface description of the person's outward activity.

The Man and His Message

Now, if a historical character leaves a written message, that message cannot be purely and simply identified with the writer. Even when the man or woman and the message complement and explain each other, they never coincide totally. Each of us possesses his/her own personality, significance, destiny, and role; but when we die, we may become the object of an interpretation over which we have no control. On the other hand, if we leave a message, that message is a view of reality, an overall vision of God, of humanity, and of the world, as well as a plan for life's journey. When such a message concerns the Christian life, it can be called a "spirituality."

But a Christian spirituality cannot be centered on any mere human, no matter how great or holy, but only on Him "who alone is holy, Jesus Christ." When a historical figure leaves behind a body of writing describing a particular vision, even a partial one, it is in those writings rather than in someone else's account of the person's life that we must look for his/her message. We must, therefore, distinguish between the person and the message. This is particularly so when it is a question of an anonymous writing, coming from an author whom we cannot identify or whose name we do not recognize. Yet we must remember the immense and lasting influence exercised by the works of such writers as Pseudo-Dionysius, or Hadewijch, the thirteenth-century Flemish mystic, about both of whom we know practically nothing. But even when the authors are outstanding, well-known personalities, it is usually the message conveyed by their writings that is better known and more influential than the authors themselves. For example, the writings of St. Irenaeus, St. Augustine, Origen, St. John of the Cross, and Angelus Silesius, to mention but a few, are not centered on their own lives, even though these writings cannot or should not be dissociated from their authors. When we study one of these works, we are more interested in the contents than in the personality of the author as such. It is true that there are some writers, especially women writers, whose message is largely autobiographical, such as Angela of Foligno, Teresa of Avila, and Thérèse of Lisieux. But even here, the author does not see herself or present herself as the focus of attention or as an example to be imitated. Her personal experience simply serves as a starting-point and basis for a spiritual doctrine that is valid for everyone.

Francis's case is, however, a special one. When we read the innumerable biographies and the countless studies of his spirituality, we get the strong impression that his message is simply himself and his way of life. For example, when F. Vandenbroucke was writing about the "Franciscan spring," he dealt with the subject of Francis's spirituality by simply retelling the Saint's life. In contrast, the usual procedure is, first, to describe briefly the person who initiated the particular spiritual movement and only then to write at length about the component parts of the movement. In the case of Francis, however, his spiritual teaching was closely linked to his personality. It is only right, therefore, that his written message should be taken into account.

Biographies of Francis: His Writings

As we know from experiences, people are sometimes surprised to learn that Francis ever wrote anything. Once, when we mentioned Francis's writings to a noted Scripture scholar, who was also well-versed in history, he was quite surprised and very skeptical. He did not believe that Francis even knew how to write, and he thought that the Saint's being regarded as an author was just pious wishful thinking. On another occasion, the editor of a learned review, a noted ecumenist, was incredulous when we told him about the work being done on Francis's writings. He wanted to know if such writings really existed, if they were genuine, and if so, did they have anything new to offer. So it is that even well-educated people may have only a vague idea of who the real Francis was and what he stood for. A hazy outline may well be all they know of the Saint's teaching. The truth is that the popular image of Francis has overshadowed his written message.

Francis was a man of incomparable charm who fascinated and left a deep impression on his own generation and, through the accounts which that generation handed down, on those who lived in the centuries that followed. The Saint's vibrant personality and universal appeal were reflected in the appearance of numerous enthusiastic biographies. In fact, some ten lives appeared in the thirteenth century alone—and that was only the beginning! Since then, in every century, people have drawn their own picture of Francis according to the way they understood him.

Until modern times, that is, until the late 1800's, the predominant image of Francis was that of a man who imitated Christ so closely that he even bore the marks of the Lord's Passion on his body. Indeed, Francis was the first stigmatist known to history. Each succeeding century added its own emphasis to this basic portrait. In the fourteenth century, a friar, Bartholomew of Pisa, stressed the Saint's resemblance to Christ so strongly that he made Francis seem like another Christ, almost equal to his divine Master. There then followed a period during which Francis's likeness to our Lord was especially accentuated, particularly as regards details of Christ's earthly life. It is easy to understand, therefore, the Lutheran reformers' reaction to this surge of enthusiasm for Francis. Indeed, Luther himself wrote the preface to a book vilifying the Franciscans.

The modern, historically-based type of biography first appeared in the late nineteenth century. Interest in Francis as a troubadour and poet of the waning Middle Ages began with the rise of romanticism in Germany. In France, this new kind of biography was vigorously promoted, mainly by F. Ozanam, E. Michelet, E. Renan, and especially by Paul Sabatier (1858-1928), who has rightly been called the "father" of modern Franciscan historical writing. Sabatier was a Protestant pastor, a liberal theologian, a distinguished historian, and an admirer of Francis. His life of the Saint was to leave its mark on all the later biographies. However, because of his background and cast of mind, Sabatier saw Francis's life as a struggle between the Saint's intuition and the dogma of the institutional Church, so that he made his biography a drama of a heroic battle between one man and a monolithic power, a battle that could lead only to the lone warrior's defeat.

Practically every life of Francis published since then, no matter how serious and learned, has, for better or worse, reflected this point of view. Every year from then on, more than one life of Francis has appeared, all unfortunately repetitive and rarely offering anything new. Such a flood of material certainly testifies to Francis's appeal to succeeding generations, who interpret the Saint's influence to suit the taste of the times. Yet they all continue to identify the man with the message.

Now, Francis left a body of writings which, while they do not teach us much about the Saint himself, do convey a distinct message. Sabatier saw that these writings, so lovingly preserved, were important for understanding and interpreting Francis's message; yet they have scarcely been used by the biographers for this purpose.

Nevertheless, P. Miccoli, the Italian medievalist, holds that the writings should provide

> the criteria and the parameters for measuring, evaluating and appreciating the distorted approaches, interpretations and translations by means of which Francis's contemporaries and their successors have seen and understood his life and teachings.

An Unusual Author

It is clear, then, that Francis's personality has eclipsed his humble written message. And his was indeed a humble message because he thought of himself as "ignorant and unlearned" (*ignorans et idiota*: EpOrd 39). However, in the Middle Ages, this did not mean "an ignorant idiot" but merely someone who had not pursued the literary and theological course of studies prescribed for the clergy.

Now, apart from women writers such as Angela of Foligno and
Catherine of Siena, all the ecclesiastical authors of antiquity and
the Middle Ages were clerics who had done approximately what
we would call "higher studies." In this respect, the only figures in
Christian antiquity comparable to Francis would be St. Anthony
the Abbot and St. Benedict, the fathers of Eastern and Western
monasticism respectively, neither of whom had had the benefit of
an advanced education.

Francis did learn to read and write, which meant that he knew
Latin, the language of literacy at the time. He received his
education in his home town of Assisi, at a school which was
comparable to a cathedral or abbey school but which was not an
"upper" or "high" school. There he undoubtedly learned more than
simply how to decipher a text. As we can see from his writings, he
had an above-average intelligence and an especially retentive
memory. But he was not shaped by the intellectual trends and
methods of his time, as well he might have been.

Like himself, the writings he has left us are also humble and
unassuming, consisting as they do of some thirty texts of varying
lengths, each occasioned by some special circumstance. In total,
they would cover only about 150 pages of an average-sized modern
book, which is quite short in comparison with the work of most
theologians and spiritual writers. This brevity, however, has the
advantage of making it feasible to examine and comment on the
texts in minute detail, which obviously is not possible in the case of
St. Augustine or St. John of the Cross, for example.

Francis, then, was a simple, unpretentious man, "uneducated
and common" (*sine litteris et idiota*), like the Apostles in the Acts
(4:13). Yet he has left us a not inconsiderable body of material,
whereas his contemporary, St. Dominic, has bequeathed us nothing
in writing, although he was a Canon Regular, educated in the
clerical schools.

Introducing the Writings

Although Francis described himself as "unlettered," he did know
how to write, for we have two texts in his own hand—the *Praises
of God* and the *Letter to Brother Leo*. On other occasions, he
dictated his thoughts to scribes who were more skillful at wielding

a pen than he was. It is surprising to see the importance he gave his writings and how insistent he was in recommending that they should be read, copied, kept, and meditated upon. He earnestly begged "all the brothers to learn the tenor and sense of these things . . . [and to] teach, learn, retain, remember and put [them] into practice" (RegNB 24:1f.). They were "to keep [them] with them" (EpRect 9; EpMin 21) and "have copies made and pass them on to others" (2EpFid 88; 1EpCust 9; EpCler 15). He expressed this desire in various ways in no less than nine of his texts; that is, in those just mentioned and in three others (1EpFid 2:20; EpOrd 47; Test 36). No wonder, then, that more or less complete collections of his writings were made from an early date. The oldest known of these compilations, the Assisi Codex 338, dates from around 1252, little more than twenty years after Francis's death, and 150 more are listed for the two following centuries. The authenticity of these writings is, therefore, well established. At the beginning of the twentieth century, in 1904, two critical editions of the writings appeared, while, in 1976-1978, K. Esser published another in two versions, major and minor, which met all the demands of modern critical scholarship.

A short introduction to the writings will be useful. Only two of the texts, the *Canticle of Brother Sun* and the *Canticle of Exhortation to St. Clare and her Sisters*, were written in the Umbrian dialect and are the first writings in Italian. The rest are in elementary, unpolished, but generally correct Latin. They differ greatly in length, from the longest, the *Earlier Rule*, which covers twenty-six pages, to the shortest, the *Letter to St. Anthony*, which contains only four lines. Between these two extremes, we have the *Office of the Passion*, arranged by Francis (eighteen pages), the *Admonitions* (eleven pages), the *Later Rule* (nine pages), the *Second Letter to the Faithful* (seven pages) and other shorter ones.

At first glance, it seems impossible to classify the writings, since they were composed for different occasions and are apparently quite unrelated to each other. However, when we examine their contents and the various reasons for which they were written, we can distinguish three categories.

The **first** category contains those texts which, in a general way, provide norms for the Gospel life, namely, the *Admonitions*, the

Salutation of the Virtues and *True and Perfect Joy*. Then there are those which, like the two versions of the *Letter to the Faithful*, are addressed especially to all Christians living in the world. Finally, there are quite a few others which describe and regulate the Gospel life of the groups which Francis had gathered together—the two *Rules* for the friars, the *Form of Life Given to St. Clare and her Sisters*, the *Rule for Hermitages*, the *Testament of Siena*, and also the *Testament* and the *Letter to the Entire Order*, although these last two were written in special circumstances.

The **second** category of writings is the prayers, most of which take the form of praise. There is no doubt that these prayers occupy a special place in Francis's writings, because, in various forms, as pieces on their own or as passages in other texts, they cover some forty pages out of a total of 150 pages. There are about twenty of these prayers, notably the striking hymn of praise in chapter 23 of the *Earlier Rule* and the mystical *Praises of God*.

The **third** category contains those texts which are official communications in the form of letters and those which are expressions of affection. The three letters mentioned above, that is, the two *Letters to the Faithful* and the *Letter to the Entire Order*, are more like short treatises than letters. Then there are the occasional writings, short messages to the clergy, the rulers, the custodians (superiors) of the friars and also personal letters, such as those to an unnamed minister (superior) of the friars, to Brother Leo and to St. Anthony, as well as tokens of affection in the form of blessings to Brother Bernard and Brother Leo.

The texts belong to various literary types. Some are short treatises, such as the *Second Letter to the Faithful*, while others legislate for, or urge others to follow, a special way of life (the *Rules*). Some of the texts are reminiscent of the sayings of the Fathers of the Desert (the *Admonitions*), while others are ardent exhortations (the *Testament, Letter to the Entire Order*, chapter 22 of the *Earlier Rule*), or prayers written in a poetic style (*Praises of God; Exhortation to the Praise of God*; chapter 23 of the *Earlier Rule*). The texts also contain legal language (*Letter to a Minister* 13-30; *Later Rule* 2:4) and even precise legislation (*Earlier Rule* 8), while the *Letter to Brother Leo* shows deep human tenderness, *True and Perfect Joy* is a dramatic narrative, and the description of a sinner's death is particularly vivid (2EpFid 72-85).

There is no serious doubt about the authenticity of these texts. The unity of their contents is immediately clear to the attentive reader, as is also the similarity of language and style. Although the Latin vocabulary used in them is relatively rich (1,800 words, which is quite a respectable number), the syntax is elementary, sometimes awkward, and even incorrect. It is noteworthy how many adjectives there are in the texts and how they are grouped into twos and threes. We are safe in assuming that Francis did not write the texts with his own hand, apart from the two mentioned above. Instead, he dictated them directly in Latin, which the scribe would correct as needed; or else he dictated them in his own Umbrian dialect of Italian, and the scribe then translated them into Latin. Some of the more carefully crafted texts, such as the *Letter to the Entire Order* and certain passages in the *Later Rule*, probably required a more active participation by the scribe, although their contents and style remain Francis's alone.

Most of the theological and spiritual writings of this period were produced by educated monastic authors, especially the Cistercians, and by university scholars, such as the Victorines. Compared with these works, Francis's texts are unusual, since they are at once both simple and profound, as we can see from his approach to his subjects and his style. He does not use long chains of logical discourse, or learned, complicated arguments, but makes simple statements, one after the other, with great conviction and restrained passion. Yet he employs few similes and metaphors and often desists from his tendency to pile one adjective on top of another, as if he is eager to get to the point he wishes to make. His writings are more concerned with people and their psychology than with the things of nature. He does not use imagery; and, although his writings can be lyrical, especially when he is praising God, and although they are often rhetorical, too, they are not particularly poetic. Even in the *Canticle of Brother Sun*, he praises God for His goodness to us and simply points to Brother Sun, Sister Moon, etc., as examples of that goodness.

Contents of the Writings

For those who are not familiar with Francis's writings, it may be helpful if we provide a quick survey of the contents of the texts, using the three categories we have outlined above.

1. In the category of **general norms for living the Gospel life**, we must first name the *Admonitions, True and Perfect Joy* and the *Salutation of the Virtues.* The *Admonitions* are a group of twenty-eight sayings or aphorisms of varying lengths, dealing with our inner attitudes towards God, our neighbor (eight Adms), and especially ourselves (seventeen Adms). They show us how insidious our selfishness is and point the way to self-abnegation, to the extreme poverty so dramatically depicted in *True and Perfect Joy.* The *Admonitions* are the charter, the Song of Songs, of the most profound Franciscan poverty: "He is blessed who does not keep anything for himself, rendering to Caesar what is Caesar's, and to God what is God's" (Adm 11).

The *Salutation of the Virtues* and Admonition 27 are lyrical about the path that leads, not to death, but to the kingdom of the virtues of wisdom and simplicity, poverty and humility, love and obedience. When we reach that kingdom, we are completely recollected, at peace in quiet acceptance of everything (*apatheia*).

The two versions of the letter to Christians living in the world (1 and 2 *Letters to the Faithful*) sketch out the Gospel way opened up by the paschal mystery of Christ. They describe the various elements of that way—the Church, the sacraments, love of neighbor, self-knowledge, and self-abnegation. They list positive features as well as negative (the death of the sinner). They celebrate the spiritual experience, the happiness, of those upon whom the Spirit of the Lord rests at the end of the road, when He takes up His abode in them and causes them to share in the communal life of the Trinity. This is one of the most mystical passages in Francis's writings, yet it does not occur in the texts intended for his friars. Instead, it is part of a letter, or tract, addressed to people living in the world.

The description and organization of the life of the friars are the subjects of several documents. There are two *Rules*, one differing slightly from the other. The earlier one, dated 1221, is longer and much richer in spiritual and scriptural explanations. Although the later one, dated 1223, is more condensed, Francis's personal touches are more clearly visible in it. The basic elements of the friars' life are listed—their bonds with the Church, prayer, fraternal life, daily duties (work, begging), radical poverty (refusal of all property and money), maintaining a peaceful, kindly presence among the people. It also lists various offices essential to the Order (ministers).

Some chapters of the *Earlier Rule* (17; 21-23) amply develop the spiritual foundations of the Gospel life—self-abnegation, openness to the mystery of God, and the message to be brought to the world. The *Rule for Hermitages* lays down the external conditions for the search for "the kingdom of God and His justice" in solitude. The *Testament of Siena* gives the three essentials of the friars' life—fraternal love, poverty, and loyalty to the Church.

Two other documents belonging to this category were occasioned by special circumstances and therefore were not intended to give an overall view of the friars' life but only to touch upon certain important elements of that life. Francis's *Testament* includes an autobiographical section, the only time the Saint speaks at any length about his spiritual journey. He briefly recounts his conversion and proclaims his faith in priests and churches. Then, in a few lines, he recalls the main characteristics of the early life of the friars. Finally, he counsels his brothers on poverty, on asking for privileges, and on obedience and finishes by setting down the way in which the *Rule* and his *Testament* are to be interpreted.

The *Letter to the Entire Order* begins with a richly theological address to the friars and goes on to deal mainly with the priest-friars' celebration of the Eucharistic liturgy. The letter continues by developing profound thoughts on the Eucharist itself and on the spiritual conditions required to be worthy of it.

The letters addressed to the Poor Ladies at the beginning of their lives at San Damiano (FormViv) and shortly before Francis's death (UltVol) show how, from the start, Francis based the Gospel of the Poor Ladies on the Trinity and surrounded them with fatherly care (CantExh).

2.   We shall now examine the category of the **prayers.** The most outstanding are the fifteen psalms of the *Office of the Passion.* In these, Francis follows the traditions of the Church and has our Lord Himself speak and pray, thus allowing us to hear the Son's heartbreaking yet trusting cry to His Father, followed by His song of victory. After this paschal prayer of pain and joy comes Christ's majestic priestly prayer, taken from chapter 17 of the Gospel of St. John, which Francis uses three times.

The *Praises to be Said at All the Hours* and the *Exhortation to the Praise of God* are two liturgically-structured invitatories in which the themes and texts are borrowed mainly from the Book of Revelation. These texts are simply mosaics of scriptural quotations ingeniously fitted together with no trace of artificiality, as is also the commentary in the *Prayer Inspired by the Our Father*, which may well be a re-working of a pre-existing text that Francis adapted to his own purposes.

The *Canticle of Brother Sun* praises the Most High Lord for the beauty and harmony of His creation, as well as for the sufferings and failures we experience and our inevitable death, all of which we accept from God's hands.

In the *Praises of God*, which Francis composed and wrote in his own hand at the time of the stigmatization, some forty of God's attributes are crowded together, jostling each other and giving us a glimpse of the writer's ardent love of the Most High. Of the prayers that occur in the middle of other texts, the most important, because of its length and its theological content, is found in chapter 23 of the *Earlier Rule*. Here, in the form of a prayer of praise and thanksgiving, Francis lyrically depicts a vision of God and humanity and retells the saga of their relationships in the world and in history. He ends this prayer with an invitation to everyone to go to meet God and to love Him above all else.

The *Prayer before the Crucifix*, which dates from the first years of Francis's conversion, expresses in a few pithy words the glory of God, the darkness of the human heart, and the paths that lead to a meeting of the two.

The prayer that ends the *Letter to the Entire Order* (EpOrd 50-52) condenses into one long sentence a spiritual journey which, by following in the footsteps of the Son and passing through the purifying fires of the Spirit, leads the faithful soul to the Most High Father.

Two beautiful texts celebrate the glory and radiance of "the virgin made church" (SalBMV 1), who is unequaled among women (AntOffPass 1). Other short prayers, invitatories, and prayers are scattered here and there among the texts.

3. The third category of texts is that containing the **letters** and expressions of affection. The most remarkable of these is the *Letter to a Minister*, in which Francis shows the freely-given, inexhaustible mercy of God—and of Francis—towards the sinner, even the unrepentant sinner.

The *Letter to Brother Leo* is a short, friendly, even "motherly" letter that is profoundly respectful of the recipient's personal path to God, while the *Letter to St. Anthony* is an assignment.

The blessings given to Brother Leo and Brother Bernard show Francis's kindness and genius for friendship. Three other letters contain practical messages. The *Letter to the Clergy* and the *First Letter to the Custodians* are concerned, first, with the respect due to the sacrament of our Lord's Body and Blood and to His written words. They then call upon all the clergy of the Church and the ministers of the friars to show this respect, giving the theological reasons why they should do so.

The powerful *Letter to the Rulers of the Peoples* reminds the rulers of their duty to God, asks them to invite their people to praise and thank God, and reminds them of the final judgment by Christ that awaits them.

Scripture in the Writings

The Old and New Testaments are the backdrop to Francis's writings. By simply counting the number of biblical quotations the Saint used, we can see how important they were to him. He quotes the Old Testament 156 times and the New 280 times, a total of 436 quotations. By comparison, the works of St. John of the Cross, which are at least ten times as long as Francis's, contain only 1,526 quotations, 907 from the Old Testament and 619 from the New. Most of Francis's quotations from the Old Testament are from the Psalms, while, from the New Testament, he quotes 146 times from the Synoptic Gospels (seventy-five from St. Matthew, fifty-eight from St. Luke, and thirteen from St. Mark), twenty-one from St. John, and fifty from St. Paul. Leaving aside the numbers, when we study Francis's understanding and use of Scripture, we can see that his vision of the Triune God, as expressed in his writings, comes from St. John, his view of humanity from St. Paul, and his rules for daily living mainly from the Synoptics.

It is clear that Francis took all his biblical quotations, fragments, and allusions from the Latin text of the Vulgate, not, however, as it is in the editions published since the Council of Trent, but as it was in common use, with many variations, in the liturgical books of his day. The breviary which he used had an appendix called an *evangelistare*, which, as the name implies, contained all the Gospels used at the time (225 different texts). It is generally accepted nowadays that he derived his knowledge of Scripture mainly from the liturgy as he heard it read, prayed, and chanted. This would indicate that he did not depend solely on sheer memorization, but that he learned from his spiritual insight into the liturgy and from the interpretation of Scripture contained in the liturgy.

It is interesting to note the types of writing in which Francis does or does not use biblical quotations. Some of his writings have no Scripture quotations at all in them, such as, among others, a part of the *Admonitions*, the *Letters to the Custodians*, the *Salutation of the Blessed Virgin Mary*, the *Salutation of the Virtues*, *True and Perfect Joy*, and the *Canticle of Brother Sun*. Other documents have very few quotations—the *Testament*, the *Rule for Hermitages*, the *Later Rule*, the *Praises of God*, the *Letter to the Clergy*, the *Letter to a Minister* and the *Letter to the Rulers of the Peoples*. On the other hand, besides the obvious example of the prayers—the *Office of the Passion*, the *Praises to be Said at all the Hours*, the *Exhortation to the Praise of God* and the *Blessing for Brother Leo*,—his five great texts make abundant use of Scripture—the *Earlier Rule*; fourteen (that is, half) of the *Admonitions*; the *First* and *Second Letters to the Faithful*; and the *Letter to the Entire Order*.

Francis, then, multiplies quotations from the Bible particularly when he is intent on providing an overall view of the Gospel life.

Francis's Use of Scripture

Francis used Scripture and integrated it into the development of his thought in original and varied ways, proving once more how familiar he was with Holy Writ. Close examination of those writings which we have cited will show that he uses as many as five different approaches to biblical quotations.

First, numerous passages in his writings were *inspired* by, or completely *permeated* with, Holy Scripture. Without using any explicit quotations, he could weave almost the whole fabric of a document from threads of biblical thoughts. Thus, for example, the passage from the *Later Rule* (3:10):

> I counsel . . . my brothers . . . that, when they go about the world, *they do not quarrel (non litigent*: see 2 Tim 2:23f.; Tit 3:2) or *fight with words (non contendant verbis*: see 2 Tim 2:14) or *judge others* (see Lk 6:37): rather, let them be *meek (mites*: see Mt 5:4), *peaceful* (Mt 5:9), *unassuming (modesti*: see 2 Tim 2:24; Tit 3:2) and *gentle (mansueti*: see 2 Tim 2:24; Tit 3:2).

There are many other passages in the same style (e.g. RegNB 21; 2EpFid 22; EpOrd 5-10).

Second, Francis sometimes quotes Scripture *explicitly* and solemnly, using introductory phrases such as: 'The Lord says . . . ,' 'The Lord commands . . . ,' 'According to the Gospel . . . .' He applies these quotations to concrete situations, or else he comments and meditates upon them.

He applies the quotations in two ways. In the first way, he takes a quotation as a basis or point of departure for an attitude or action. There are four instances of this in the *Earlier Rule* (3:1f.; 8:12; 16:1f.; 22:1f.):

The Lord says: *This kind* of devil *cannot come out except* by fasting and *by prayer* (Mk 9:28), and again, *When you fast, do not become sad like the hypocrites* (Mt 6:16). For this reason, all the brothers . . . should celebrate the Divine Office. . . . Similarly, all the brothers should fast (RegNB 3:1f.).

At other times and more frequently (for example, in RegNB 2:10; 4:5f.; 9:1, 13f.; 16:7-9; 22:6f.; RegB 9:3; 2EpFid 16-21; EpOrd 15f.), he uses a quotation by way of confirmation, justification, or conclusion of a development of thought. Thus the brothers are asked:

to have humility, patience in persecution and weakness, and to love those who persecute us, find fault with us, or rebuke us, because the Lord says: *Love your enemies, and pray for those who persecute and slander you* (Mt 5:44). *Blessed are those who suffer persecution for the sake of justice for theirs is the kingdom of heaven* (Mt 5:10: RegB 10:9f.).

Third, those Scripture quotations upon which Francis comments or meditates occur especially in the *Admonitions*: there are eleven of them (Adm 2-5, 7-9, 13-16). He emphasizes a word or phrase, as from three Beatitudes—the poor (Adm 14), the peacemakers (Adms 13,15), and the pure of heart (Adm 16)—and uses it as a subject of meditation rather than as a point of departure towards a practical conclusion. In his meditative passages, he describes a situation or an inner attitude but does so in a contemplative vein:

I did not come to be served but to serve (Mt 10:28), says the Lord. Those who are placed over others should glory only as much as they would were they assigned the task of washing the feet of the brothers. And the more they are upset about their office of [washing] feet, so much the more do they store up treasures to the peril of their souls (Jn 12:6) (Adm 4).

An especially notable example of this process occurs in the *Prayer Inspired by the Our Father*, where Francis meditates at length on each petition of the Lord's Prayer.

The **fourth** way in which he uses Scripture is by harmonizing quotations, that is, by using parallel passages. In this, he takes a whole passage or part of one from a Gospel, and, in the case of one of the three Synoptic Gospels (that is, Matthew, Mark, or Luke), he completes or parallels it with the other Synoptics.

There are three examples of this in chapter 22 of the *Earlier Rule*: the parable of the sower, the return of the unclean spirit, and Christ's priestly prayer (Jn 17:1-26). The first two examples follow St. Luke's Gospel in the main—the sower (8:11-15), the unclean spirit (11:14-25)—but he also uses the parallel passages from Mark (4:14-20) and Matthew (13:19-23; 12:43-45). In the third example of harmonization, he quotes from the priestly prayer of John 17:1-26 three times in his writings—in the *First* and *Second Letters to the Faithful* (1EpFid 1,14-19; 2EpFid 56-60) and in chapter 22 of the *Earlier Rule* (22:41-55).

In the first two examples of harmonization, Francis is concerned about preserving the richness of the Synoptic Gospels, whereas, in the third example, he goes further and amplifies the priestly prayer. Out of the twenty-six Gospel verses which he uses in the *Letters to the Faithful*, seven are from the priestly prayer, while, in the *Earlier Rule*, there are seventeen verses from the prayer, showing his clear preference for that Gospel passage.

The **fifth** way in which Francis uses Scripture is to group together verses or fragments of verses taken from different books of the Bible and centered around a single theme. These groups may loosely be called *florilegia*, that is, collections or anthologies, although they are not comprehensive enough to deserve that name. There are seven of these groups in the writings, five of them being in the *Earlier Rule*, while the other two are in the first section of Admonition 1 (1-6), the *Praises to be Said at all the Hours*, and the *Exhortation to the Praise of God*.

The theme of the first group is the following of Christ, what it demands and what it promises (RegNB 1:2-5). This group is made up of four different quotations. The theme of the second group is the manner in which one should conduct oneself with other people (RegNB 14:1-5—six verses). In the third group, nine quotations, one after the other, describe the attitude to maintain in trials and persecutions (RegNB 16:11-21). In chapter 22 of the same *Rule*, two very elaborate groups occur, one after the other, on adoration with a pure heart (22:27-31), and on the shepherd who gathers his flock together (22:32-40). The first of these two groups contains five quotations, the second eight. The better to illustrate Francis's method, we give here the complete passage on adoration in spirit and truth:

> Let us make a home and dwelling place (see Jn 14:23; Eph 2:22) for him . . . who says: Watch, therefore, praying constantly that you may be considered worthy to escape all the evils that are to come and to stand secure before the Son of Man (Lk 21:36). And when you stand to pray (Mk 11:25), say: Our Father who are in heaven (Mt 6:9) And let us adore Him with a pure heart, because we should pray always and not lose heart (Lk 18:1), for the Father seeks such worshippers. God is spirit, and those who worship Him must worship Him in spirit and in truth (Jn 4:23f.).

We must also include here the *Office of the Passion*, another especially important group of psalms which Francis composed to celebrate the paschal mystery and the coming of Christ in history and at the end of time. This "office" contains fifteen psalms, of which thirteen are formed from psalms and other biblical texts, while the remaining two are given exactly as they are in the psalter. This ingenious, artistic arrangement shows that Francis possessed unusual spiritual insight and considerable literary ability.

It is immediately apparent from the different ways in which Francis used Scripture that he had an exceptional knowledge of the Word of God. His major writings were, naturally, the ones that were most his own because he expended most effort on them. Yet, basically, they are simply the proclamation of God's Word, especially of the Gospels, with some little commentary. Contrary to popular opinion, Francis's Gospel spirituality is not narrow and restricted and does not consist merely in knowing and putting into practice some radical directives about poverty. Instead, he had a wide and comprehensive grasp of the whole message of salvation.

His way of introducing and commenting on biblical texts owes nothing to the complex methods of interpretation of his own day.

He never uses the allegorical or the accommodated senses of Scripture, except perhaps in the *Later Rule* (9:4): *verbum abbreviatum:* "in few words" (see Rom 9:28; Is 10:23; EpOrd 19, on the text of Jer 48:10) as well as in certain psalms. Everything in his writings is direct, simple, and straightforward. A modern Scripture scholar will feel more at home with Francis's approach to Holy Writ than with the way most of the spiritual works of the Middle Ages and later epochs used it. Francis's "exegesis" or interpretation of Scripture can be compared to that of St. Basil in his Rules and, much closer to our own day, to that of St. Thérèse of Lisieux. His interpretation may be literal, but it penetrates to the heart of the text, thus avoiding mere surface literalism. The *Admonition* which deals with the letter that kills and the spirit that gives life shows the true nature of Francis's understanding of Holy Writ:

> Those are given life by the spirit of Sacred Scripture who do not refer to themselves any text which they know or seek to know, but, by word and example, return everything to the most high Lord God to whom every good thing belongs (Adm 7:4).

Elsewhere in the *Admonitions*, he speaks about "the pleasure and joy" which are to be found in "the most holy words and deeds of the Lord," with which we can "lead people to the love of God in joy and gladness" (Adm 20:1f.).

That is the invigorating atmosphere we find in reading Francis's interpretation of Scripture.

Other Influences

Scripture was the principal, not to say the only, source of the vision that inspired Francis's writings. He came to understand and absorb the Word of God through the liturgy in its various forms—praise, proclamation and chant—so that his knowledge of the Bible was both profound and balanced. Were there any other factors that influenced his writings? We cannot deny that the radical poverty movements of the twelfth century, such as the Waldensians, the Humiliati, the hermits, and the wandering bands of preachers, may have created a climate that had its effect on Francis. In the *Earlier Rule*, there are eight Gospel texts which are also quoted in the Humiliati's *Propositum*, approved by Pope Innocent III in 1201, while the title "minister" ("servant") was given to the superior of that group. Admonition 27 has echoes of Camaldolese spirituality, while the *Earlier Rule*, when speaking about work and idleness, quotes the Rule of St. Benedict and the words of St. Jerome and St. Gregory the Great (RegNB 7:10-12). Again, the phrases that Francis uses—"the life of the Gospel" *(vita evangelii)* and "to observe the holy Gospel" *(observare evangelium*: RegNB Prol:2; RegB 1:1)—rather than the more usual "apostolic life" *(vita apostolica)*, are reminiscent of the Rule for the Order of Grandmont drawn up by Stephen of Muret (died 1124).

Apart from these, we can detect no other factor that could have had a direct influence on Francis or of which he showed conscious signs. Nor can we discern in his writings any traces of Cistercian spirituality, whose great exponents, William of St. Thierry (died 1148) and St. Bernard (died 1153), lived near his own time and who did influence St. Clare. The Victorine school did not influence him nor did the current concept of the mystical marriage *(Nonnen-mystik)*. Moreover, a comparison between Francis's writings and the Constitutions of the Order of Preachers, which can be regarded as a "twin" of the Franciscan Order, demonstrates clearly that they come from two very different currents of spiritual thought.

Francis stands out as an unusual personage among all the main characters involved in the spiritual movements of ancient Christianity, that is, in the origin and development of monasticism and in the various movements in the Middle Ages. He was a layman with no scholastic background, who was little influenced by the scholarly currents of his times. Despite all that, he bequeathed to us a relatively important written message which, as we shall see, was very rich in content. Without reference to the story of his life, we can find in his writings the paradox of divine wisdom combined with "littleness" and weakness.

Dating the Writings

Although we have examined the writings and classified them according to their themes, we have not yet tried to date them. That is what we shall attempt now. Obviously, the writings were composed during a definite time-span, that is, during Francis's lifetime, short as it was. His literary activity, if we may use that rather pretentious term in his case, lasted for about twenty years at most, and it is not easy to fix precisely the dates of the various writings within that period. Between the first of his compositions, which was undoubtedly his *Prayer Before the Crucifix* (about 1206), and the last texts, the *Testament of Siena* and his *Testament* (in 1226), about twenty years passed. But where, in that span of time, are we to place each of his other writings?

Part of the Rule which he presented to Pope Innocent III in 1209 is still to be found in the *Earlier Rule*. The *Form of Life Given to St. Clare and her Sisters*, which is so rich in theology, dates from the years 1213 to 1215; and the *First Letter to the Faithful*, in which he developed similar mystical themes, must have followed soon after.

But most of his writings were composed just before and after 1221—the *Letter to the Clergy* and the *Letters to the Custodians* about 1220; the completion of the *Earlier Rule*, the composition of the *Later Rule*, and the *Praises of God* in 1224; the *Letter to the Entire Order* and the *Canticle of Brother Sun* about 1225. The *Admonitions* presuppose an intense spiritual experience and great spiritual maturity, which Francis was able to condense in short, pithy formulas, so that this text must be placed around the same date, 1225.

We can perceive an evolution in the sequence of writings about certain practical matters, such as obedience, work, and idleness, for example. But it is more delicate and difficult to detect the development of Francis's theological and spiritual insight. We find that some themes—for example, the Trinitarian dimension of the Christian life—occur very early in the writings, as they did in the *Form of Life Given to St. Clare and her Sisters*, which appeared around 1215. And, later on, Francis took up the same themes again and developed them further—for example, in the *First* and *Second Letters to the Faithful*, the *Earlier Rule* (chap. 22), and the Antiphon in the *Office of the Passion*. His broad vision of salvation history (cf. the *Earlier Rule*, 23:1-6) is a mature work, although it was composed before 1221. Here again we cannot but be amazed at the rapid, brilliant spiritual concentration which Francis displayed in his writings, the work of the Spirit of God in a man who was simple yet highly gifted by nature.

Contemporary History in the Writings

We are not trying here to describe the historical context, that is, the political, social, cultural, and ecclesiastical climate of the times in which Francis lived, but rather to find out if, and to what extent, his writings reflect those times. We have already made a clear distinction between the biographies of Francis and his own written message. These biographies, especially the modern ones, depict in greater or less detail the world of Francis's day and his involvement in it. In contrast, his writings were devoted mainly to Gospel realities, to theological and spiritual matters. Nevertheless, they do carry echoes about the people, situations, and circumstances of the thirteenth century.

Although his writings are by no means centered on Francis himself, he does figure in them. He writes about "Brother Francis"—never just "Francis"—and says that he is "a worthless and weak man" (EpOrd 3), "a useless man and unworthy creature of the Lord God" (EpOrd 47). He mentions himself by name some nineteen times, and he speaks in the first person seventeen times in the two *Rules* and elsewhere (2EpFid, Test, EpOrd, EpMin, EpLeo). The *Testament* is partly autobiographical, and from it we learn about his state of ill-health (cf. also 2EpFid, EpOrd, TestSen). But he makes few such concrete references to himself; and if all we knew about his life was what he tells us in his writings, we would know very little indeed about him.

On the other hand, we learn something about his personality and psychology from the way he addressed others and how he often included himself by saying "we" instead of "you." He was very human, even tender, often calling his companions "my blessed brothers," who were "worthy of respect and much loved." He offers "homage and reverence" to the Christians of the world, and, when writing to the rulers of the peoples, he calls himself "your little, despicable servant." He knew how to use a whole range of emotions in his appeals, going from simple exhortation, through insistent imploring and impassioned pleading, to brisk commands. He could be authoritative, even authoritarian. The abrupt "I command" and the imperious "I wish" occur several times in the *Testament* alone; and in some passages he seems almost angry (EpOrd 44; Test 31-33).

We know the names and circumstance of some friars who were close to him—Leo, Bernard, and Anthony. The *Rules* give an impersonal description of the conduct required of those who joined the religious group. The brothers had to sell their possessions, wear the religious habit, sever family ties, live on the margins of society by sometimes sharing the lot of the poorest people, do manual labor under orders from others, beg when necessary, and be willing to be despised by others while not despising them in return. They were to tend the sick and were told how to act towards those who welcomed them with kindness and those who rejected them.

The *Rules* did not turn a blind eye to the evils that threatened the community. The brothers would be tempted to judge and despise others, to be puffed up with spiritual pride, to cast off the yoke of obedience, to eat and drink to excess, to allow themselves to give in to sloth, to collect money despite their vow of poverty, and to lapse into fornication. Thus Francis did not merely hold up the ideals for which they should strive, but also accurately assessed the concrete situation and pointed out the dangers that threatened those ideals.

The world outside the Fraternity also appears in the writings—the Popes, Innocent III and Honorius III, the cardinals, the bishops, the clergy in general and priests in particular, as well as the religious; and even the theologians are mentioned explicitly (Test 13).

Then there were the people in general—men and women, cleric and lay people alike. In a remarkable text (RegNB 23:7), Francis lists the numerous social classes of the time. On the one hand, there are the well-dressed, well-fed wealthy people (RegB 2:17), still attached to their possessions even on their deathbeds (2EpFid 72-81). On the other hand, there are the "people [who are considered to be] of little worth and who are looked down upon, . . . the poor and the powerless, the sick and the lepers, and the beggars by the wayside" (RegNB 9:2).

Francis also knew the important men who governed the city-states—the "mayors and consuls, magistrates and rulers" (EpRect 1); and he referred to "the masters of Paris" and the kings of two emerging nation-states, "the king of France and the king of England" (VPLaet 5). Beyond the quite extensive Christian world, there were "the Saracens and other nonbelievers" (RegNB 16:2;

RegB 12:1; VPLaet 6), among whom Francis and his brothers wished to go, "not to engage in arguments and disputes, but to be subject to every human creature for God's sake" (RegNB 16:6).

And while it is true that Francis lived in the middle of the internal conflicts of his own city, Assisi, and the frequent armed clashes between the cities of the region, he makes no direct reference to this state of affairs in his writings. He reacted to the prevailing climate of hostility, not by resorting to violent denunciation and bitter argument, but by proposing a different kind of life, a "counter-culture" based on the Gospel.

Francis's writings are essentially spiritual, and by that very fact may seem to be totally unconcerned with temporal affairs. However, those writings, like similar works of the time, were inevitably affected by their historical context; and so, discreetly but no less certainly, Francis's written words contain echoes of that context, reveal several aspects of it, and reflect the actual situation of the times.

Reading and Interpreting the Writings

Before attempting to obtain a comprehensive view of the message in the writings, we must read carefully and make a detailed interpretation of each text if we are to avoid generalizations and subjective assessments. Such a project was courageously undertaken only about fifty years ago. In theory, the importance of Francis's writings has always been seen and acknowledged, and this is especially true since the time of P. Sabatier. However, no serious study or judicious use of the writings was made as a means of understanding and presenting the Saint's message.

The pioneer in this field was Kajetan Esser, OFM, a German Franciscan, who published a university thesis in 1947 on Francis's *Testament*. Twenty years later, in 1967, one of Esser's pupils, David Flood, OFM, produced a similar piece of research on the *Earlier Rule*. Some of Francis's other writings were later studied scientifically; for example, the *Letter to the Clergy*, by B. Cornet, in 1955; the *Rule for Hermitages*, by K. Esser, in 1962; the *Later Rule*, also by Esser, in 1969; the *Office of the Passion*, by L. Gallant, in 1978; the *Letter to the Entire Order*, by O. Schmucki, in 1980; the

Admonitions, by P. Brunette, in 1990; and numerous studies on the *Canticle of Brother Sun*, such as that by E. Leclerc, in 1970.

These are only some of the more outstanding authors, and many more scholars have worked on the same texts. With the exception of the two *Letters to the Faithful*, all the major texts have been researched, while partial studies have been carried out on one or other chapter or passage from the writings, especially of the *Earlier Rule*. C. Paolazzi has written a study of all the writings together. So, gradually, by learning to understand the different parts of each text and each text as a whole, scholars have laid a solid foundation which is being built on by research conducted in various places and by different university faculties, but especially in the Institute for Franciscan studies in Rome.

When all the texts have been minutely studied and classified, it will be possible to concentrate on particular points or themes. In this area, S. Verhey has done pioneer work on Francis's anthropology; and, in 1973, a Vietnamese Franciscan, N. Nguyen-Van-Khanh, submitted to the Catholic Institute in Paris a thesis sponsored by Père Chenu, entitled "Jesus Christ in the Thought and Writings of St. Francis" (translated into English by Ed Hagman, OFMCap, and published under the title, *The Teacher of His Heart*, [St. Bonaventure , NY: The Franciscan Institute, 1994]). Since then, other monographs dealing with various themes have appeared— for example, on the universalist traits in Francis's prayers by L. Lehmann in 1984; on his anthropology by Gniecki in 1987; on "The Humility of God" by J. B. Freyer in 1989; and on the concept of priesthood by Holter in 1992. Due mainly to the pioneer work of O. Van Asseldonk, many studies of Francis's interpretation of Scripture and the way he read and understood the Gospel have been published. Two such studies deserve special mention—a book by W. Viviani (1983) on Francis's interpretation of St. John and a remarkable exegetical study by D. Dozzi (1989), dealing with the use of the Gospel in the *Earlier Rule*.

The way has now been cleared for discerning the comprehensive, global vision which is surely to be found, either explicitly or at least implicitly, in Francis's writings.

The Possibility of a Comprehensive View

Everybody agrees that there is such a thing as Franciscan spirituality, that is, a certain way of viewing and living Christian and human values, a way that owes its origins to Francis and the spiritual movement he began. When authors tried to find the source and the essential elements of Franciscan spirituality and how these elements fit and work together, they inevitably turned first to Francis's own life, as we have already noted. The result was a rather haphazard mixture consisting mainly of extracts from the old biographies of the Saint (used without much critical discernment), combined with some of his writings, and then presented as part of a study of the spiritual theologians of the Middle Ages. This approach did have some value, especially in so far as it handed on traditions and living experiences.

But surely we should be able to share to some degree in Francis's comprehensive vision of God and humanity without necessarily having recourse to his many biographies and their varying interpretations of his life. Everything we have said in the preceding pages shows that this is indeed possible and encourages us to attempt it.

Besides teaching exegetics, I have applied myself for many years to reading and interpreting Francis's writings, keeping up, as far as possible, with the numerous books and articles devoted to them. In an article in *Sources chrétiennes* ("Vision qui se dégage des écrits de François," pp. 49-81), I attempted to outline a comprehensive overview of Francis's writings; and I have continued my research by means of lectures, courses, and published articles. As my investigation progressed, I saw that it would be worth my while to expand, hopefully with more maturity, what I had already sketched out.

Despite the diversity of Francis's writings and their fragmentary nature, I came to the conclusion that they all stemmed from a unified, structured vision. Since the writings are relatively few in number, each one of them can be subjected to a close exegetical examination in order to see what unifies them. My study of particular themes has helped me to avoid a subjective approach and has shown me the richness of Francis's thought, which is sometimes hidden but is more often readily discernible. Of course, there is no question here of hoping to find an elaborate, well-developed system of thought in the Saint's writings. But, as one historian has remarked: "It is surprising to find [in Francis's writings] substantial unity of content and form" (L. Pellegrini: *Francesco*, p. 327). We can, therefore, share another historian's hope of achieving "a systematic presentation of Francis's writings" (A. Rotzetter: *Franziskusdeutung*, p. 137).

But since there is no apparent system in the writings, we are faced with a difficulty when attempting to present a comprehensive overview. How can we avoid adopting "a method of synthesizing which is more or less inspired by that of the medieval *Summas*," as we have been accused of doing in *Sources chrétiennes*? In fact, instead of imposing a framework from outside, we must find, in the body of the writings themselves, a key, a parameter, a unifying idea that links together and explains their scattered elements.

In an endeavor to present the nucleus of Franciscanism, G. Minotti thought he had found the key in the *Testament*. Strictly speaking, his conclusion is tenable when applied to the life of the friars themselves. However, because the *Testament* is essentially an "occasional" document, written in particular circumstances, it does not cast sufficient light on the central elements in the life of the brothers. In any event, the scope of the *Testament* is too narrow to provide a comprehensive vision of the theology and spiritual teaching in the body of the writings.

After a long search, I reached the conclusion that the writings offer two examples which can be taken as a key to a complete overview of their message. Those examples are: chapter 23 of the *Earlier Rule* and the *Second Letter to the Faithful*. This *Rule* offers a full, dynamic picture of God, humanity, and history, while the *Letter* traces out a path based on knowing and following Christ, the Second Person of the Blessed Trinity. These two texts open up an approach to other documents, such as chapter 21 of the *Earlier Rule* and Admonition 1, and help us to find the full meaning and unity of various scattered passages. This is so because it is in the *Earlier Rule* and the *Second Letter to the Faithful* especially that we find the best expression and adaptation of Francis's global concept of reality, visible and invisible, of "all things spiritual and corporal" (RegNB 23:1).

Limitations

Like any other personal project, ours has its limitations. We should like to present a coherent overview that would take account of all the literary, theological, and anthropological riches in Francis's writings. However, we are aware that such an ambition can be realized only in part because the writings are open to different readings and hence different interpretations—literary, historical, theological, and semantic. The ideal would be to use every one of these approaches, but to do so would mean mastering them all and using them properly. Instead, we shall simply employ what Scripture scholars call the historico-critical method, while stressing the theological and spiritual dimension, which, from all the evidence, is at the source of the writings, as we hope to show.

Ignoring the theological and spiritual elements of Francis's work leads to incomplete, biased representations of his message. Other methods have been tried; for example, D. Flood focused mainly on the social aspect of Francis's plan, while E. Leclerc and P. Bonnette took the Jungian psychological approach. The method we prefer is not the only one available, but we believe that it is fundamental to a true assessment of Francis's teaching. Instead of analyzing each text and putting each into its own context, we propose to form a comprehensive overview of them all. We shall inevitably run the risk of reducing everything to one point of view, or making the writings fit into a logical framework imposed from outside, or claiming to be completely objective. We are aware of these pitfalls and wish to avoid them but have no assurance that we shall do so entirely.

There are two aspects of the writings which immediately present difficulties, namely, their relative brevity and the almost total absence of a consciously coordinated system of thought. Yet, even starting from such a narrow base, we believe that it will be possible to reach a global understanding of Francis's theology and of his views on humanity and the Christian life. But will the result contain, and be in complete harmony with, the whole of Christian revelation about God and humanity? In other words, will

Francis's writings show that he was a master of the spiritual life, the founder of a spiritual movement, who expressed in an original way the whole width and depth and balance of the Christian vision? Our conviction, based on protracted study of his writings, is that they will.

Nevertheless, we do not claim that Francis said everything there is to say, nor do we wish to compare him with such giants as Augustine, Gregory of Nyssa, and John of the Cross. Still, while his writings are neither elaborate nor voluminous, they do have a Gospel freshness and immediacy and do not lack some of St. John the Evangelist's theological depth and the drama of St. Paul. Like his sister from Lisieux, he was one of the little ones, "the babes," to whom God revealed His love and that of His Son (Mt 11:25f) and who delight in repeating what they have seen.

Although Francis is rightly regarded as one of the greatest of the Saints, he is never thought of as a mystic or theologian. But, as the Fathers of the Church understood the terms, a *mystic* is someone who discovers and penetrates into the mystery of God and His works, while a *theologian* discerns and contemplates the depths of visible and invisible reality. In the patristic sense, then, Francis was both a mystic and a theologian.

From what his writings allow us to glimpse, we can conclude that Francis taught an authentic spirituality centered on the Triune God and not on himself, as so many biographers mistakenly think. We shall try to demonstrate this point of view.

Chapter 2

Keys to Reading Francis

In the preceding chapter, we distinguished between Francis and his message and briefly introduced that message, which we showed to be the essence of his spiritual vision. Then we asked if this vision was a unified and coherent one. In fact, Francis does not describe his vision as such in any one text, for, as we saw, all his writings are occasional and fragmentary. Must we, then, just do the best we can by first studying the numerous themes that emerge from the writings and then gather these themes into groups, as the old textbooks used to do with the "tracts" in theology, thus fitting them into an artificial framework? Fortunately, close examination of the writings shows that two of them provide a comprehensive overview of Francis's vision, namely, chapter 23 of the *Earlier Rule* and the principal passages in the *Second Letter to the Faithful*.

Here we propose to introduce and analyze these two texts in order to show what they have to say about God, humanity, and the spiritual life. That done, we shall follow the same line of inquiry in the other writings. Our findings should enable us to combine the essential points from all the writings in a comprehensive overview in which there is no hint of artificiality.

Francis's *Credo* (RegNB 23:1-6)

The *Earlier Rule* is the longest of Francis's writings, and it ends in an unusual fashion, with a lengthy prayer and an impassioned plea to the whole world. It certainly was not the Saint's custom to insert in a law-making text a long prayer which was addressed to God alone and which, moreover, did not concern the friars directly. This section of the *Rule* must have been very dear to Francis because he lingered so long over it and used it as a glorious finale to the plan of the Gospel life which he proposed to his brothers. It is amazing to find such passion and poetry, such richness and yet such balance in this type of *Credo*.

We shall first give the whole text and then try to indicate its main and subsidiary trains of thought:

1. All-powerful, most holy, most high and supreme God, Holy and just Father, Lord, King of heaven and earth, *we thank you* for yourself, for, through your holy will and through your only Son, with the Holy Spirit, you have created all things spiritual and corporal, and, having made us in your own image and likeness, you placed us in paradise. 2. And through our own fault we have fallen. 3. And *we thank you*, for, as through your Son you created us, so also, through your holy love, with which you loved us, you brought about His birth as true God and true man by the glorious, ever-virgin, most blessed, holy Mary, and you willed to redeem us captives through His cross and blood and death. 4. And *we thank you*, for your Son Himself will come again in the glory of His majesty to send the wicked ones who have not done penance and who have not known you into the eternal fire, and to say to all those who have known you and have adored you and have served you in penance: "Come, you blessed of my Father, receive the kingdom which has been prepared for you from the beginning of the world!" 5. And because all of us wretches and sinners are not worthy to pronounce your name, we humbly ask that our Lord Jesus Christ, your beloved Son, in whom you were well pleased, together with the Holy Spirit, the Paraclete, *give you thanks*, as it pleases you and Him, for everything, He who always satisfies you in everything, through whom you have done such great things for us. Alleluia! 6. And through your love, we humbly beg the glorious Mother, most blessed Mary ever-virgin, blessed Michael, Gabriel and Raphael, and all the blessed choirs of seraphim, cherubim, thrones, dominations, principalities, powers, virtues, angels, archangels, blessed John the Baptist, John the Evangelist, Peter, Paul, and the blessed patriarchs, prophets, the Innocents, apostles, evangelists, disciples, martyrs, confessors, virgins, the blessed Elijah and Henoch, and all the saints who were, who will be and who are *to give you thanks* for these things, as it pleases you, the supreme and true God, eternal and living with your most beloved Son, our Lord Jesus Christ, and the Holy Spirit, the Paraclete, world without end. Amen. Alleluia.

This is evidently a text composed with great care, a true work of art, very like some of the Eastern anaphoras of St. Basil. (Broadly speaking, the anaphoras were the equivalent of the modern Eucharistic Prayers). The three prayers of thanksgiving addressed to the Father unfold before our eyes the great work of our salvation. When we behold such an outpouring of "holy love," our human language falters.

Only God Himself can praise God worthily and give proper thanks for the magnificence of His gifts (vv.1-4). That is why Francis calls upon the Son and the Paraclete to take up the paean of praise which we have intoned (v.5). Then follows the third movement of the symphony (v.6), in which the Communion of Saints, led by Mary and the angels, is called to join in the hymn of thanksgiving sung by the beloved Son, accompanied by the Holy Spirit.

Thus, we, the people of today and every day, even though we are sinners "with unclean hearts," join in the eternal hymn of thanksgiving of the Son and the Holy Spirit, as the glorious procession of those who are saved passes before us.

The structure of this passage from the *Earlier Rule* is a remarkable achievement for "a little poor man" like Francis, but even more noteworthy still are its contents. The passage, the prayer, is so completely and unwaveringly centered on God and humanity and provides so many perspectives on both that it is difficult to say which of the two is its main focus. It refers to the Trinity, to Christ, and to the universe, and its vision is dynamic, historical, and ecclesial. Finally, it is cast in the form of a hymn of thanksgiving to the Trinity. All the elements in it are bound together in a profound unity.

The prayer takes its main points from the *Credo*. It professes belief in, and gives thanks to, the Almighty Creator, proclaims the Incarnation and the Redemption by the Son, and looks to His return in glory. It evokes the presence of the Spirit, the Church, saints and sinners. Nevertheless, one feature stands out immediately, the prominent place we humans occupy in the whole scheme of things. The *Credo* proclaims the mystery of the Trinity and enlarges on the part the Son plays in everything. We humans appear there only in passing on the occasion of the Incarnation and the Passion: "for *us* and for our salvation, He came down from heaven. . . . He was crucified for *us*." On the other hand, however, we can say that, in Francis's prayer, we are as present in each strophe as God Himself is.

In one sense, this act of thanksgiving singles us out particularly as the focus of God's loving attention, "of the holy love with which He loved us." We are first envisaged in all our extraordinary grandeur: we are the object of divine love, the crowning glory of creation, the image and likeness of God, and we are destined for the happiness of heaven. It is true that we have been degraded by sin and have become its captives, that we are wretched sinners, unworthy even to utter God's holy name. Yet the Son will restore us to the paradise we have lost, provided only that we do not refuse to go to Him. He will lead us into "the kingdom prepared from the beginning." Even now, we can sing out our wonder and acknowledgment. Side by side with us sinners, there appears the world of glory, the world of those "who were, who will be, and who are" saved.

The prayer is centered on us, our destiny, and our vocation, but, at the same time, it is even more focused on God. Francis's attitude towards humanity is rooted in, and rests solidly upon, his knowledge of God and is inseparable from it. When he speaks about us men and women, he always sees us as the objects of God's eternal will. God keeps us always in mind and wishes to have us with Him, and so we say to Him: "We thank you for yourself," that is, we thank God for being God (cf. EpOrd 50).

Francis, the contemplative, gazes on God and, in awestruck wonder, glimpses something of the divine immensity. And what he sees is not a shapeless shadow but God's "holy will" and "holy love" for us. He knows that this abyss of love is waiting to receive us, that God really loves us and, in some mysterious way, cannot do without us. This God, whose majesty Francis evokes by piling term upon term—ten in all—this God is no longer an abstract deity but is the "holy and just" Father of Jesus Christ. The vision of God which Francis has is resolutely *trinitarian*. His thanksgiving is addressed to the Father alone, for it is He who takes the initiative in everything. The *Credo* places Christ at the center of His own mysteries, but in Francis's prayer, the Father not only "created all things" but also "brought about [His] Son's birth" and redeemed us through Christ's Passion. Thus Francis attributes the Incarnation, the Redemption, and the Second Coming of Christ to the Father: these are His works. The Son is only, as it were, carrying out His Father's will, a view that is closely akin to the perspectives of the Gospel of St. John.

Surprisingly, the Son and the Spirit, whom Francis asks to intervene in giving thanks to the Father, seem to be subordinated to the Father. Here and in other texts, as we shall see, Francis stresses the centrality of the Father—He is the sole Origin of the internal communion of the divine mystery from which the Son and the Spirit spring and to which they flow back. We could call this "an unorthodox subordination" in the relationships in the Trinity in which the Father holds the primacy, the "monarchy" (*monarchos*: "ruling alone"). But the Son and the Holy Spirit also appear with the Father, acting with Him "like two hands" in the work of creation, in the redeeming Incarnation, in the Second Coming (of the Son alone) and in the thanksgiving which They are invited to render to the Father.

Francis also emphasizes the christological dimension. The beloved Son in "whom [the Father was] well pleased" and "who always satisfies [the Father] in everything" is at the Father's side at each stage of the act of thanksgiving. With the Father, Christ creates "all things spiritual and corporal," including us men and women. It was out of love for us that the Father "brought about" the birth of Christ "as true God and true man" and "willed to redeem us . . . through His . . . death." Christ will come in the name of the Father, "in the glory of His majesty," to bring those "who have known" God into the "kingdom . . . prepared for [them] from the beginning of the world." He, the beloved Son, is the proof of the Father's love for us, and He alone knows the song of thanksgiving that is worthy of the Father. Even the heavenly choir, led by "the glorious Mother, most blessed Mary" and composed of all that is good and noble in humankind, cannot praise the Father as He deserves, if they are not motivated and inspired by the "beloved Son together with the Holy Spirit, the Paraclete."

Although the role of the Spirit at first seems less evident here, He, too, takes part in the creation, so much so that "the holy love" which urged the Father to act with the Son in the Incarnation and Redemption, may well be Francis's way of alluding to the omnipotence and omnipresence of love which is the Holy Spirit. Similarly, in the act of thanksgiving in the two last strophes of the prayer, the Spirit is always joined with the Son and, like Him, is turned towards the Father.

Francis's prayer also has a *cosmic*, universal aspect since God is the Creator of "all things spiritual and corporal." This is the only time Francis mentions material things in his prayer, but we must not forget that we humans who dominate the scene are the first of those "corporal" things, as is also the Son "made man." We should note that Francis includes in his global vision the material universe which he also celebrates elsewhere, especially but not exclusively, in his *Canticle of Brother Sun*.

Francis's prayer is dynamic. It has movement, for it does not simply contemplate static figures but tells a story. It is a "theological narrative." In fact, it is in the same literary line as salvation history when it proclaims the great works of God. Everything begins with creation, conceived in the mind of God ("for yourself") and carried out by His incomparable design ("through your holy will"). Spirits, the heavenly bodies, and human beings made in the image of God are all destined for happiness. This is prologue. Then comes the Fall, the result of the sin of our first parents, followed by the Son's being sent in the flesh for our redemption. Finally (eschatologically), comes the glorious consummation of all at the end of time. It is the Father who has given us everything and continues to do so, for it is He "who created us and redeemed us and *will save* (the future tense) us by His mercy alone (RegNB 23:8). So, contemplating the Father in the whole broad sweep of His works, Francis calls Him by the all-embracing titles, "Creator and Redeemer and Savior" (RegNB 23:9,11), to which he would later add the title, "Consoler" (ExpPat 1).

The angels and saints named in the long final list are part of this consummation, which is both the beginning and the end, the *alpha* and the *omega*, that which was and that which will be. We men and women of today are situated between these two poles in a kind of permanent present. Francis's plural "we" is like a thread that runs through the whole fabric of his prayer. Strangely, this "we" concerns the present (which is normal) as well as the past. It is *we* who have been created, been placed in paradise and fallen. It is *we* who have been freed from the slavery of sin. It is for *us* that the kingdom was prepared "from the beginning of the world," that kingdom which we have lost but whose gates remain open to us. We can therefore understand better our inability to give proper thanks to our Creator and see the reason why Francis begged Him to come to our aid by expressing our gratitude in His own language, the Word made flesh, and with His own breath, the Holy Spirit.

Because we normally use the singular "I" when praying, Francis's use of the plural "we" in his prayer is somewhat surprising. However, we must note that he uses "we" in almost all the prayers preserved in his writings. The one who is speaking here is not a solitary, isolated individual but is part of a collective history, a member of a group, of the Church or even of the human race. We can, therefore, speak about the ecclesial, "churchly" character of Francis's vision. In it, all humanity stands before God, recalls its history and sings its hymn of thanksgiving to Him. Humanity in the form of the Church is at once glorious in its origin and destiny but wretched and sinful because of its fall. It is glorious because a whole procession "of those who were" has already reached final glory. Leading this procession is "most blessed Mary"; then come the heavenly spirits with their leaders; next, the greatest names among the Saints; then the anonymous litany in which are listed all the classes of those who have been saved; and finally "the two saints of the last days," Elijah and Henoch.

This is a vision of beauty, of overflowing abundance. God is Beauty and Beneficence. He shows the profundity of His Being in the inner life of the Trinity and the harmony of His works, which unfold like a drama in which surprises and reversals are not lacking, a divine drama, a "theodrama." Every reversal is seen in the light of "the holy will" and the vision of heaven, because, after the Fall, and after "the cross and blood and death," we shall be made whole in the new paradise which those "blessed of the Father" are invited to enter. When Francis beholds this vision of God's work, he can only sing out with "joy and gladness" (Adm 20). His contemplation and his language take on an *aesthetic* form. He gazes on Him whom he twice calls "Beauty" (LaudDei 4) and, in order to speak of Him, uses a lyrical version of the Eucharistic doxology. But Francis was "an unlearned man" and did not know the Eastern Eucharistic anaphoras in general or that of St. Basil in particular, or indeed anything similar in the Western tradition. Yet he was able simply and spontaneously to use language that was as rich and as appropriate as theirs.

At first we are inclined to ask if it is indeed possible to find any kind of unified vision in Francis's writings, fragmentary and occasional as they are. But then we are surprised to find such a vision succinctly expressed in this short, closely written text which we have been studying, a text which, in addition, is poetic. This document will serve as a kind of pattern or model which we can use to assemble the various elements of Francis's vision that are scattered here and there throughout his writings. He had a global, unified image of God and humanity as well as of salvation history, in which they interacted, and it is this image that will be our guide in our research.

We should like to point out another passage in Francis's writings which conveys the same global message but which develops further the christological dimension of his vision. This passage is found in the "doctrinal" introduction to the *Second Letter to the Faithful* (vv.2-15). Here Francis also envisages the mysteries of Christ, the Incarnation, the Pasch that is performed in the Eucharist, the Garden of Gethsemane, and the Passion. In this passage the Father is as truly present as the Son and the presence of the Holy Spirit looms large. This solidly theological text proposes the following of Christ as the foundation of the Christian life. We shall deal with this particular point later, after we have considered the mystery of Christ.

A Program for the Christian Life

The nearest thing to a theological treatise or tract that Francis wrote was undoubtedly his relatively lengthy *Second Letter to the Faithful*. It was the result of a process of evolution, since Francis probably first composed it around 1216-1218 in a short, impersonal form without addressing it to anyone in particular and with a final recommendation written in the plural. After 1221-1222, he took it up again, expanded the introduction greatly, addressing it to a specific group and closing with a theological perspective. He also added important developments that resulted in a kind of program for the Christian life which he suggested to all convinced Christians in general, a sort of embryonic *Introduction to the Devout Life*. The more "mystical" parts—for example, the closeness to the Trinity promised to the faithful Christian—are identical in the two versions of the *Letter* (1EpFid 1:5-13; 2EpFid 48-56) and bear witness to the early maturing of Francis's deep spiritual insight.

While the *Earlier Rule* (23:1-6) provided an overview of Francis's image of God and His plan for our salvation, this *Letter* lists and describes the modes of conduct required by the Gospel life preached by Christ. The *Earlier Rule* was concerned with the theology of salvation, while the *Letter* deals with living the Gospel life in order to attain that salvation. Although the *Letter* is not a "summary" of the Gospel, it does give the requirements for living the Gospel life and once again describes vividly its rewards in heaven. It is important to note that these requirements—and their rewards—are not reserved for a special type of person, such as friars and nuns. They are set before "all Christian religious—that is, those who are trying to live their Christian life to the full— clergy and laity, men and women, and . . . all who live in the whole world" (2EpFid 1). The path that Francis is tracing out here is simply the normal Christian way of life, and the heights to which it leads are accessible to everyone.

We are not going to reproduce the *Letter* in its entirety here. We shall deal first with the introduction and then go on to consider the main points, which give an outline of what Francis understood to be the Gospel life, that is, the Christian life lived to the full.

Foundation: the Father Sends the Word

Before giving in detail the demands of the Christian life, Francis lays the solid foundation on which it rests: theology precedes morality, the gift precedes the commandments. As in chapter 23 of the *Earlier Rule*, we have here a concise exposition of the doctrine of the Trinity but this time dealing more explicitly with the role of Christ in our redemption. Francis does not retell all of salvation history but only Christ's intervention and how that intervention is perpetuated in the Eucharist.

Here is the text:

1. Since I am the servant of all, I am obliged to serve all and to administer to them the fragrant words of my Lord. Therefore . . . I have proposed to set before you in this present letter and message the words of our Lord Jesus Christ, who is the Word of the Father, and the words of the Holy Spirit, which are spirit and life. 2. Through His angel, St. Gabriel, the most high Father in heaven announced this Word of the Father—so worthy, so holy and glorious, in the womb of the holy and glorious Virgin Mary, from which He received the flesh of humanity and our frailty. Though He was rich beyond all other things, in this world He, together with the most blessed Virgin, His mother, willed to choose poverty. 3. And, as the Passion drew near, He celebrated the Passover with His disciples, and, taking bread, gave thanks, and blessed and broke it, saying: Take and eat: this is my body. And taking the cup, He said: This is my blood of the new covenant which will be shed for you and for many for the forgiveness of sins. 4. Then He prayed to His Father, saying: Father, if it is possible, let this cup pass from me. And His sweat became as drops of blood falling on the ground. Nonetheless, He placed His will at the will of the Father, saying: Father, let your will be done, not as I will, but as you will. 5. And the will of the Father was such that His blessed and glorious Son, whom He gave to us and who was born for us, should, through His own blood, offer Himself as a sacrifice and oblation on the altar of the cross, not for Himself through whom all things were made, but for our sins, leaving us an example that we should follow in His footsteps. 6. And the Father wills that all of us should be saved through Him and that we receive Him with our pure heart and chaste body. But there are few who wish to receive Him and be saved by Him, although His yoke is sweet and His burden light.

The first thing that catches our attention in this passage is the frequency with which Francis uses the word *verbum*, "word"—five times in three verses, and the title "Father" applied to God (eight times). Thus, from the beginning, he is using the "fragrant words" with which he is "obliged to serve all." These, however, are not his own words but those of Christ and the Holy Spirit, and so they are living words, capable of giving "spirit and life" (Jn 6:64). From this, we can see the lessons which Francis wants to teach in this letter and which he boldly identifies with the Gospel word. But this Gospel word is only the verbal expression of Him who, in His very Being, is the Word, the *Verbum*, of the Father, who is distinct from Him. The development that follows plays upon the two terms, the "Father" and His "Word."

It is the Father who sent into the Virgin's womb this Word, "so worthy, so holy and glorious." In Mary's womb, the Word "emptied Himself" by receiving "the flesh of humanity and our frailty" and "though He was rich beyond all other things, He, together with the most blessed Virgin, His mother, willed to choose poverty." Christ chose to take on the poverty of our human nature as well as material poverty during His sojourn on earth. From the Incarnation, the text goes quickly to the Passover, which "as the Passion drew near, He celebrated . . . with His disciples." Like a Eucharistic Prayer, Francis's letter solemnly and lovingly repeats the whole account of the institution of the Eucharist, thus marking the importance that the mystery of the Body and Blood of Christ has in his vision of Christ's work in the world.

Even though the Son, through whom all things are done, is "worthy, glorious and holy," Francis's christology stresses the painful aspects of His life—the choice of weakness and poverty as He came into the world, His agony and bloody sweat in the Garden of Gethsemane during His Passion, the confrontation between the two wills, the Father's and the Son's. The Father wished that His "blessed and glorious Son . . . should, through His own blood offer Himself as a sacrifice," while the Son asked to be spared such a fate, but, nevertheless, "placed His will at the will of the Father." The result of this self-abnegation by the Son is that we are freed from sin, and Christ is held up to us as a model in whose footsteps we should follow.

The last passage in this section of the letter (v.6) makes the connection between the contemplation of the mystery of Christ's self-emptying and the conduct proposed to the Christian. The

Word was sent by the Father and was in constant dialogue with Him. The Blessed Sacrament sums up everything that Christ accomplished, "not for Himself, but for us" for whom He was born and to whom He has been given. That is why Francis stressed the institution of the Eucharist in his christology: "The Father wills that all of us should be saved through Him and that we receive Him . . . (because) His yoke is sweet and His burden light" (vv.14f.).

The demands that follow (v.16) are neither possible nor meaningful unless they are rooted in this gift of the Father, who again takes the initiative, of the Son who gives Himself and the Spirit who alone helps us to worship "in spirit and in truth." Thus the rules of conduct proposed by Francis are based on what the Father has done for us in Christ, "whose yoke is sweet and whose burden is light" (14).

Welcoming Christ and Being Saved by Him

The rest of the *Second Letter* is devoted to describing what we must do if we wish to respond to God's gracious gifts to us in His Son. The first version of the *Letter* (1EpFid 1:1-4) had already laid down five requirements in a few compact sentences—to love the Lord God, love our neighbors, renounce our sinful selves, receive the Eucharist and "produce worthy fruits of penance." The *Second Letter* takes up these points, develops them considerably and adds others, thus providing a complete plan for the Christian life.

The transition from one version to the other, from theoretical theology to practical rules of conduct, is marked by Francis's using the language of the Beatitudes to describe the happiness of those who welcome the gifts of God in Christ: "How happy and blessed are those who do not . . . refuse to taste and see how sweet the Lord is," who love the light rather than the darkness, "who fulfill the commands of God," especially the command to love God and neighbor (cf. 2EpFid 16,18).

Francis develops this teaching at length in four parts. First, he lays down the basic requirements for the Christian life (vv.19-36); then, he lists the demands of the interior life (vv.37-47). Next, he paints a glowing picture of the rewards in store for those who "have done such things" (vv.48-60); and, finally, he utters a joyous cry of praise of God (vv.61f.).

The Gospel Way

The basic elements of the Christian life are: the believer's relationship with God; the sacramental life; conversion of heart expressed in love of neighbor and self-restraint; and, lastly, fidelity to the Church.

The first requirement is found in the Gospel text about the twofold commandment of love of God and neighbor (Mt 22:37-39). Francis immediately associates love of God with adoration, which is the action of "a pure heart and a pure mind, because He . . . seeks this above all else" from those who adore Him. This interior attitude will be manifested when we "praise Him and pray to Him, day and night," a prayer and praise that is summed up in the Our Father. In this way, we shall be able to pray always (vv.19-21).

The second demand is sacramental (vv.22-24) and brings us into the profound mystery of the Church. We must confess our sins to a priest and receive the Body and Blood of our Lord, without whom we cannot enter the kingdom of God. But, as St. Paul warns us, we must do so while "discerning the body" of the Lord (1Cor 11:29).

Then we are told that we must do as the Gospel tells us and "perform worthy fruits of penance" (cf. Lk 3:8). This was important to Francis because we find it in two other places in his writings (RegNB 21:3; 1EpFid 1:4). Our conversion, our new way of life and conduct which this phrase describes is shown especially by our love of neighbor (vv.26-31): "Let us love our neighbors as ourselves." To which Francis adds with keen psychological insight: "If there is anyone who does not wish to love them as himself, at least let him do no harm to them, but rather do good."

The way we express this love in action will vary according to our position in life and our opportunities. Those who have the responsibility and the power to decide and judge—for example, priests, magistrates, and superiors—shall do so with mercy. But Francis admonishes all of us to be humble and not to dominate or be overbearing in our relationships with our neighbors. Instead, we should learn how to share what we have by giving alms. Another "fruit of penance" is asceticism, personal self-control, both spiritual and corporal: "We must also fast and abstain from vices and sins and from any excess of food and drink" (v.32).

We are to demonstrate our fidelity to the Church by "be[ing] Catholics," an attitude which Francis describes at some length. First, we must do something that seems quite ordinary but which was especially dear to Francis's heart: "We must also visit churches frequently" (v.33; Test 4,18). Furthermore, it is most important to keep in touch with the Church, represented by "the clergy," by "venerat[ing] and show[ing] respect" for them, "not so much for them personally if they are sinners, but by reason of the most holy Body and Blood of Christ . . . and [His] holy words which [they] pronounce [and] proclaim" (vv.32-35).

Having put in place the four pillars upon which the Christian life is built, Francis goes on to lay down a series of basic interior demands which must guide the lives of those who have turned their backs on "the world." These seven principles apply to all who are resolved "to do more and greater things" and whom Francis therefore calls "religious" (vv.36-47). They are: self-denial, love of enemies, observing the whole Gospel, holy obedience, spiritual wisdom, self-contempt, and being "subject to all."

Those to whom Francis addressed this *Second Letter to the Faithful* were known in the Middle Ages as "penitents" or even "religious," that is, Christians who had resolved to live the Gospel fully without leaving their accustomed state in life. He reminded them that they were not to "leave undone" their other duties while trying to fulfill all the requirements he had listed.

In the first place, as the *Letter* will again remind us later, we have to take into account the evils which "proceed from the [human] heart," their source (cf. Mk 7:23), and which result in "vices and sins." Evil is part of our sinful selves, of "the body," or, as St. Paul calls it, "the flesh"; and we have to realize that "we must hate our bodies." Strangely enough, Francis connects this duty of hating our bodies with that of loving our enemies (v.38; cf.RegNB 22:1-8). It is the whole Gospel, "the commands and counsels," which we must observe without making exceptions and distinctions.

The life of obedience, which Francis considers at some length, is concerned with the relationships within the Christian community (vv.40-44). He tells us not to put ourselves first, to "deny ourselves," and to accept the constraints of common life, placing "our bodies under the yoke of service and holy obedience, as each one has promised to the Lord." However, there are certain limits to this, because "no one is to be obliged to obey another in anything by which a sin or a crime is committed." "The one to whom obedience has been entrusted [a perfect description of a superior!]—should be as the lesser and the servant of the other brothers." (This title "brothers" was not confined to members of a religious order). The superior should be motivated by "mercy": he should empathize with others by putting himself in their place, admonishing and supporting them with all patience and humility, and never becoming "angry with a brother."

There is a false wisdom, "the wisdom of this world and the prudence of the flesh," which Francis describes elsewhere as consisting of words rather than of deeds, outward appearances rather inner convictions (RegNB 17:10-13). On the contrary, true wisdom is a kind of *apatheia*, that is, being "simple, humble and pure" (v.45). This true wisdom is accompanied by the acknowledgment of our own profound wretchedness, which Francis stresses here and elsewhere (RegNB 22:6;23:8). He reminds us forcefully that we are "rotten, miserable . . . worms," and, by this use of the term "worm" from Ps 21:7, he identifies us with Christ, who was "made to be sin" for our sake (2Cor 5:21).

Finally, Francis returns to the attitude of submission and service which he has already outlined in his demands on obedience: "We must never desire to be over others, rather that we must be servants and subject to every human creature for God's sake" (v.47). His closing words on this matter are an invitation to us to take on the condition of Him who became the Servant of us all.

Francis uses the forceful phrase "we must" some ten times in giving his instructions, which are centered around two basic requirements. He admonishes us to reject all self-seeking and to place ourselves at the service of others, no matter who they are, to love and serve them in all simplicity, humility, and purity of heart.

The End of the Road

What will happen to those "men and women" —notice that Francis uses "inclusive" language!—who "have done these things and persevered to the end"? In one of the most "mystical" passages in his writings, he tells of the coming of the Holy Spirit to "rest" upon them and "dwell among them," giving them access to the life of the Trinity:

> And upon all [those] men and women . . . the Spirit of the Lord will rest, and He will make His home and dwelling among them. They will be children of the heavenly Father whose works they do. And they are spouses, brothers and mothers of our Lord Jesus Christ (vv.48-50).

This densely packed passage has parallels in one of Francis's prayers to the Blessed Virgin (AntOffPass) and in the *Form of Life Given to St. Clare and her Sisters.* In it, there are echoes of several Scripture texts: the sending of the Spirit upon a messianic figure (Is 11:2); St. John on the coming of the Father and the Son upon those who love Them ("We will come to him and make our home with him": Jn 14:23); an allusion to the Epistle to the Ephesians which mentions "a dwelling place *(habitaculum)* of God in the Spirit" (Eph 2:22); the bridegroom in John's Gospel (3:29); and Christ's words: "Here are my mother and my brethren" (Mk 3:34). Francis follows St. Paul's train of thought rather than St. John's and attributes the initial role, if not the principal one, to the Spirit and to His resting on the faithful Christian. When the Spirit has taken up His dwelling in us, He allows us to share in the community of the Trinity. We become "children of the heavenly Father," "spouses, brothers and mothers of our Lord Jesus Christ." This is the highest and most joyous spiritual experience we can have in this life.

Francis then adds more detail, giving the precise meaning of being a child of the Father and the implications of our threefold relationship with Christ. He can scarcely find words to express his gratitude for such happiness. He uses the exclamatory "Oh!" three times and heaps adjective upon adjective, fifteen in all, to express something of what we feel when God dwells in us. Of all Francis's writings, this is one of the rare texts, if not the only one, in which he directly expresses his own personal reaction to the touch of grace.

The *Second Letter* began by contemplating the sending of the Word and His Passion, and it ends with a twofold prayer. First comes Christ's prayer from St. John's Gospel (chapter 17), in which the Lord prays for those who are His, asking that they may be where He is, to share in His glory. Then, in an invitatory with liturgical overtones, Francis concludes his plan of the Gospel journey, beginning with the Passover with Christ and leading up to the mystery of the indwelling of the Trinity. He next gives practical directions for Christian conduct, for the "Gospel morality" which is the means of reaching God, from whom those directions come and in whom they end. The radical nature of the Christian life is based on the radical nature of God's love for us.

With the sure touch of the inspired teacher, Francis first describes the route taken by those who "love God and do what He asks." Then, in the two version of his *Letter to the Faithful*, he outlines the journey in the opposite direction taken by those "who are not living in penance" and who, "deceived by the devil, . . . are blind, for they do not see the true light, our Lord Jesus Christ." And they are foolish, "since they do not possess the Son of God, who is the true wisdom of the Father" (1EpFid 2:1-18; 2EpFid 63-85). This counter-journey begins with the rejection of the gift of salvation and loses itself in the labyrinth of selfishness, of "vice and sin and . . . concupiscence and evil desires," avarice and final impenitence. This can only lead to a "bitter death" and abandonment by God and man. That is how Francis teaches the faithful about the two ways—one which leads towards and one which leads away from the Father.

A Comprehensive View

Having examined the two texts, Francis's *Credo*, in chapter 23 of his *Earlier Rule* (RegNB 23:1-6) and the main parts of his *Letters to the Faithful*, we can say that his writings are not mere separate fragments with a few brilliant insights scattered about here and there in them. Although these two passages are not structured theological expositions or learned studies on human behavior, they do give a coherent, unified overview of Francis's thought in the form of hymns, as is the case especially in his *Credo*.

By following as closely as possible the structure of these two texts, we can present the elements of Francis's vision, or, more precisely, the actors in this sacred drama—God and humanity. We can observe the interchange between them and their insertion into the world and its history. We shall devote the following chapters to this investigation.

Part II

God and Humanity

Chapter 3

The Trinity

On every page of Francis's writings, we encounter the omnipresence of God. Whether Francis simply uses the term "God" (219 times) or, more frequently, the title "Lord" (364 times), God is the central Reality from whom everything comes and towards whom everything converges. Yet He is not an abstract, ill-defined deity, for Francis always sees and proclaims Him as the Triune God, the Trinity. This title, the Trinity, is not just an empty, theoretical formula but a term that indicates the interior divine life while stressing the "monarchy" of the Father, who always takes the first place. Here we shall consider how Francis saw God the Father as the Center and Source of everything and also how he understood the interior relationships in the Trinity as well as God's interventions in the world.

God, Whose Name "No One is Worthy to Mention"

When for the third time Francis quotes from Christ's prayer in chapter 17 of St. John's Gospel (RegNB 22:41), he says with some emotion that Christ "humbled Himself to ask His Father for us and to make His name known to us." What is this "name," this glimpse into the Father's Being which the Son gave us? Francis knew that we humans can never plumb the depths of the divine abyss designated by this generic term, "name," and in two places in his writings, he declares that "no man is worthy to mention" God's name (CantSol 2; RegNB 23:5). We are not worthy to do so because, morally, we are "wretches and sinners" but also because of our radical incapacity to know God as He is and to speak adequately about Him.

That is the paradox. Francis here seems to be advocating silent adoration as our only approach to God, yet not only does he speak at length about God (see Adm 1; RegNB 21-23; LaudDei; LaudHor), but in two other passages he also uses many terms to describe Him (RegNB 23:9-11; LaudDei). We find that he lists as many as eighty-six different divine qualities, both nouns (forty-one) and adjectives (forty-five), in an attempt to suggest something of God's ineffability. This litany of God's attributes occurs in the ardent prayer, the *Praises of God*, which Francis wrote with his own hand after he had received the stigmata. In this prayer, he uses sixty terms, one after the other, to describe "the Lord, the only God, . . . holy Father, the King of heaven and earth. . . ." He employs the same device on the last page of his *Earlier Rule* (RegNB 23:9-11), where he uses as many as fifty different terms to describe God. We get the impression that, every time Francis speaks about God, we are being allowed to catch a glimpse, a very fleeting glimpse, of the divine beauty (cf. Ex 33:23), which he tries but fails to convey by accumulating words.

He speaks about God, he stresses the way we must adore Him who is worthy of all praise, infinitely delightful yet always impenetrable to our eyes. He tells us no fewer than fifteen times that we must *adore* God, that we must approach Him with "fear and trembling," prostrating ourselves at least in spirit before His mystery. And that is so because God is, to use Francis's own words, "the Lord, most holy, most high and supreme, holy and just, all-powerful, glorious, wonderful, sublime, He who is worthy of being honored, revered and served." This adoration is so important that Francis twice quotes the text from St. John's Gospel about worshipping the Father "in spirit and truth" (RegNB 22:31; 2EpFid 19; Jn 4:23f.). Only the Spirit who "searches . . . even the depths of God" (1Cor 2:10) can teach us what our attitude should be when we are confronted with the mystery of God. As Francis perceives God, then, He is not at first a familiar, approachable Father, but the God of majesty, the thrice-holy One revealed to Isaiah (Is 6:3; LaudHor 1).

Adoration moves us to *praise* because God is "worthy to be praised and glorified forever" (cf. LaudDei). The prayers in Francis's writings are almost exclusively prayers of praise, doxologies prolonged after the fashion of the Eastern Christians. Of a total of fifteen such prayers only three contain petitions, while the remaining twelve consist solely of praise, blessing, thanksgiving, or awestruck contemplation. Francis's vocabulary of praise is markedly varied and abundant—"praising, blessing, giving thanks, exalting, magnifying, glorifying." He ends one prayer in a kind of ecstasy: "May we give you all praise, all glory, all thanks, all honor, all blessing and all good things. Amen" (LaudHor 11).

While Francis sees God the Father first and foremost as "all high, almighty," nevertheless he also stresses the other facet of the divine mystery. Because God is "delectable and totally desirable above all else" (RegNB 23:11), He is our pleasure, our absolute delight, the source of all our happiness. Francis attributes to God a whole series of qualities, some of them connected with love, since He is love, charity. There are other divine qualities, which we can call God's "attitudes" towards us, and which Francis expresses in six Latin words that are difficult to translate—*pius*, "merciful"; *mitis*, "gentle"; *suavis*, "delectable"; *dulcis*, "sweet"; *benignus*, "kind"; *mansuetus*, "meek" (RegNB 23:9-11).

God is also "good," supremely benevolent, and Francis uses this word "good" in reference to God nine times, in various contexts. Surprisingly, he says that God is "innocent." He also calls God "beauty, calm, refreshment (*refrigerium*), strength and power (*fortitudo, virtus*)," and the guardian and defender of those who place their trust in Him. We are not surprised to find Francis saying that God is "our hope and joy"—and all of this in the litany of the *Praises of God*. God's approach to us is therefore the greatest joy that can come to us whom nothing should "please," nothing "delight" except God. Thus, like all the saints, Francis takes for granted a kind of "hedonism" or pleasure seeking, in the spiritual life, but a seeking for pleasure the sole object of which is God, "the delightful."

Although God is the object of adoration, praise, and delight, He is still "beyond all things." He is beyond human knowledge, language, and experience and therefore cannot be represented by an image for idolatrous worship. Before Francis describes the sweetness of Him who, in the closing words of chapter 23 of the *Earlier Rule*, is "gentle, lovable, delectable and totally desirable above all else" (RegNB 23:11), he lists God's "negative" attributes: He is "*without* beginning and *without* end, *un*changeable, *in*visible,

*in*describable, *in*effable, *in*comprehensible, *un*fathomable." These
eight terms transcend the boundaries of all the categories into
which we might try to force God: time—He is without beginning,
without end, and without change; the senses—He is invisible;
language—He is ineffable; intellect—He is incomprehensible,
unfathomable. God remains a mystery beyond our grasp, because, as
Francis says in the words of Scripture: "The Father lives in
inaccessible light" (Adm 1:5), "God is spirit" (Jn 4;24), and "No one
has ever seen God" (Jn 1:18). It has often been said that Francis
made accessible and human the majestic God of the cathedrals.
Perhaps; but he did so without lifting the veil off the divine
mystery, as these texts prove.

Perfect Trinity and Simple Unity

When Francis is speaking about God, he rarely uses the word "God"
alone but normally puts it into the context of the Trinity. For
example, the expression, "Trinity and Unity," appears in different
forms. "Perfect Trinity and simple Unity" (EpOrd 52) occurs five
times, while the formula "Father, Son, and Holy Spirit" is used
either in liturgical praise (fifteen times)—for example, "In the
name of the Father . . . ," "Glory be to the Father . . . ,"—and in
blessings or by itself (ten times).

A sample "exhortation and praise" which Francis suggests for
use by the friars begins with the solemn invitation to honor the
Trinity:

> Fear and honor, praise and bless, give thanks and adore in
> Trinity and Unity, the Father and the Son and the Holy
> Spirit, the Creator of all (RegNB 21:2).

Here again we have the succession of adoration and praise, rising
to a crescendo with the explicit mention of the mystery of the
Trinity. The phrase "perfect Trinity and simple Unity," which
Francis uses as a kind of liturgical refrain, shows his deep insight
into the "otherness" which characterizes the relationships between the Divine Persons but which does not impinge in any way on
their "simple Unity." In the Trinity, there is perfect Diversity
within the total Unity.

The Primacy of the Father

Francis's custom of referring to the Trinity almost every time he speaks about God does not displace the Father from the center. The texts in which Francis either invokes God or speaks about Him at length are explicitly directed to the Father. Thus, in the thanksgiving in chapter 24 of the *Earlier Rule*, he calls the Father "Holy and just Father" (Jn 17:11,25), "Lord of heaven and earth" (Mt 11:25). In this way he combines the titles by which Christ refers to God in the two Gospels. He repeats almost the same words in the *Praises of God*: "Holy Father, the King of heaven and earth" (LaudDei 2).

Admonition 1 stresses the Father-Son relationship. The Father "lives in inaccessible light" and "cannot be seen except in the Spirit." The prayer at the end of the *Letter to the Entire Order* (50-52), without using the name of the Father, speaks about the beloved Son and the Spirit, who lead us "to you, Most High, who live and reign in perfect Trinity and simple Unity, and are glorified."

Francis uses the title "Father" ninety-two times in his writings, over and above the eight times he mentions the Our Father. With the exception of three passages in which he speaks about an earthly father, he always uses the title to refer to God. We must emphasize one particular point here because it has important theological consequences: Francis puts the word "Father" in Christ's mouth twenty-six times, especially in the psalms, when the Son addresses His Father or speaks about Him.

In fact, when Francis calls God "Father," he does not associate the title primarily with us but with God "the Father of our Lord Jesus Christ" (2Cor 1:3), the Father of the Son. That is to say, Francis contemplates the fatherhood of God at its very source, in the Son's relationship with the Father. He finds this relationship in the Son's prayer, especially in two particular biblical texts: in the majestic prayer of the great High Priest and Savior (Jn 17) and in the pain-filled but trusting "dialogue" between the Father and the Son in Gethsemane (Mt 26:36-46). In both of these instances, the Son glorifies the Father, conforms His will to that of the Father, and abandons Himself to the Father. In the psalms which Francis composed to follow the Passion of the Lord and in which he

amplifies Christ's two prayers, he hears the voice of the Son in
agony, speaking with His Father. Here he uses the title "Father"
fourteen times and, except in one case, he does so to make clear the
filial nature of the dialogue, to stress the Father-Son relationship
and to give the dialogue additional reverence and tenderness.

God is the Father because He begot the Son, and that is why
the Son is "beloved"—*dilectus* (ten times), "dearest"—*carissimus*,
and "blessed" (a term which Francis uses to express tenderness):
"Your beloved Son, in whom you are well pleased, . . . who always
satisfies you in everything" (RegNB 23:5). From Christ's priestly
prayer in St. John's Gospel, Francis selects two verses that recall
the Father's love for His only-begotten Son: "You have loved them
as you have loved me, . . . so that the love with which you have
loved me may be in them" (RegNB 22:53f.). Faithful to the Bible
and the traditions of the Fathers, Francis saw the fatherhood of
God as directly connected with the Trinity and only indirectly
with humanity.

As the Sole Origin, the Sole Principle, the Father takes the
initiative in everything. In chapter 24 of the *Earlier Rule*, Francis
emphasizes the fact that it was the Father who created the
universe and humanity, who brought about the birth of the Son,
who redeemed us through the Son's death, and who will have the
Son return in glory. All the divine attributes belong to the Father:
He is the Creator, Redeemer, and Savior, possessing even those
attributes that are usually assigned to the Son and the Holy Spirit
(ExpPat 6; RegNB 23:9). He is separate, apart. The Son and the
Holy Spirit appear in second place as Francis invites them to give
thanks to the Father as it pleases Him. Francis expands this
viewpoint at length in the introduction to his *Second Letter to the
Faithful*, which, while it is centered on Christ, always starts from
the Father and unfolds in His presence. He is "the most high
Father in heaven," who, through the angel, announces the coming
of the Word in the womb of the Virgin. Francis gives a brief
account, first, of the Son's coming in "the flesh of humanity and our
frailty" and then of the events at the Last Supper before going on to
describe the touching "dialogue" between the Father and the Son in
the Agony in the Garden. The title, "Father," occurs five times in
three verses of the *Letter* (2EpFid 8,10f.). As the hour of His

Passion draws near, the Son begs His Father to take the cup from Him but "He placed His will at the will of His Father." Verse 11 tersely recounts, not only the Son's sacrifice, but also the drama of the Father's gift of His Son to us: "The will of the Father was that His blessed and glorious Son, whom He gave to us, . . . [should] offer Himself as a sacrifice . . . for our sins."

In the *Salutation of the Blessed Virgin Mary*, Francis once more gives the initiative to the Father in choosing and consecrating Mary in order to make her the "home" of God. In Admonition 5, v.1, Francis speaks about the Father's creative work, for it is He who creates and forms humankind in the image of His beloved Son. Admonition 1 takes the same viewpoint: the invisible, inaccessible Father is the center to which only the Son, who is "the way," can lead us.

This movement of the Father out towards the world is always "through [His] only Son with the Holy Spirit" (RegNB 23:1) and can be understood only because of "the holy love, with which [He] loved us" (RegNB 23:3). In accordance with New Testament usage, God is here seen as love (*caritas*, used six times, four of which are quotations from the First Letter of St. John 4:16: "God is love"). Of the sixteen times the word *amor* ("love") is used, thirteen speak of God's love for us. We can understand better the mysterious expression, "for yourself" (*propter temetipsum*: RegNB 23:1; EpOrd 50), when we consider it in the context of the unfathomable abyss of God's love. Here, Francis stresses the Father's love for His Son, His other Self, and this same movement of love reaches out to embrace all of us humans.

The Father, Our Happiness

Already in this life, with God's help, we can lay aside our worldly concerns, keep our hearts pure and allow the Spirit to rest upon us to "make [in us] a home and dwelling place for the Lord God Almighty, Father and Son and Holy Spirit" (RegNB 22:27; 2EpFid 48). In this way, we become children of our heavenly Father, following His directions and acting as He wishes us to. Like Mary, "the daughter and the servant of the most high and supreme King and Father of heaven" (AntOffPass), like Clare and her sisters, who bear the same titles as Mary (FormViv 1), and as "children of the heavenly Father" (2EpFid 49), we can sing out our joy: "Oh, how glorious it is, how holy and great, to have a Father in heaven!" (2EpFid 54).

But while we are still here on earth, our knowledge of the Father is hazy and fragmentary. In his *Prayer Inspired by the Our Father*, Francis tells us that "our most holy Father [is] light . . . [and] love . . . [and is] in the angels and the saints, . . . enlightening them. . . . inflaming them to love, . . . and filling them with happiness." As for us, we ask that His name be blessed and that we may gain more knowledge of the "breadth . . . length . . . height . . . [and] depth" of His mystery as Father. But it is only when the Father brings us "to [His] kingdom" that we shall at last have "an unclouded vision . . . a perfect love . . . a blessed companionship . . . [and] an eternal enjoyment" of Him.

God is the central figure in Francis's writings, but always under the title of God the Father. It is towards His Father that the Son's gaze is directed. It is the Father's name that the Son reveals to us. He pronounces that name with tender respect: "My Father"—or, as Francis puts it, *Mi pater*, reversing the order of words in Mt 26:39, *Pater mi*, a name which the Son repeatedly invokes in His priestly prayer. So, when Francis prays to God, as the Son taught him to, he mostly addresses the Father. Of Francis's fifteen prayers, eleven are to the Father, two to Christ. and two in praise of Mary.

Francis prays to the Father, at the heart of the Trinity, the Origin of all activity, to whom everything returns. We find the best account of Francis's vision of God in the final prayer of the *Letter to the Entire Order*:

> Almighty, eternal, just and merciful God, grant us in our misery the grace to do for you alone what we know you want us to do, and always to desire what pleases you. Thus, inwardly cleansed, interiorly enlightened, and inflamed by the fire of the Holy Spirit, may we be able to follow in the footsteps of your beloved Son, our Lord, Jesus Christ. And by your grace alone, may we make our way to you, Most High, who live and rule in perfect Trinity and simple Unity, and are glorified, God all-powerful, forever and ever.

The "almighty, eternal, just and merciful" God, "the Most High who live[s] and rule[s] in perfect Trinity and simple Unity," has a beloved Son and is therefore a Father, although Francis does not use this title here. "In our misery," we address our prayers to God with the certainty that He will answer us "for" (propter) Himself and "by [His] grace alone." Here Francis traces the journey we must take, a journey during which our human actions, dependent on God, must be accompanied by our readiness to be "inwardly cleansed, interiorly enlightened, and inflamed by the fire of the Holy Spirit." Our guides on this journey are the Holy Spirit and the beloved Son, so that, "inflamed by the fire of the Holy Spirit," we will "be able to follow in the footsteps of [the] beloved Son" to the throne of the "Most High" Father. Making "our way to [Him]" is the ultimate object of our journey. While love "for" Himself (cf. "for yourself": propter temetipsum) causes the Father to reach out to His work in the world, in the end that love also gathers everything in to Itself. The Alpha is also the Omega.

The contents of this vision of God, the manner in which Francis presents it, the style of his language, the lyrical atmosphere surrounding the praise of the Trinity, and the echoes of St. John the Evangelist's theology are all redolent of the Eastern liturgies.

"The Word of the Father, so worthy, so holy and glorious"

God is a Father, who has an only Son "in whom [He is] well pleased, . . . who always satisfies Him in everything" (RegNB 23:5), and who is "blessed and glorious" (2EpFid 11). Between the Father and the Son there is an ineffable love: "Thou hast loved me . . . . The love with which thou hast loved me . . . ."(Jn 17:23,26; RegNB 22:53f.). Yet the Father does not keep the Son to Himself: "His blessed and glorious Son, whom He gave us and who was born for us" (2EpFid 11; RegNB 23:3) because of His "holy love" for us.

Francis's commentary on the fourth petition of the Our Father gives a terse description of the Father's gift to the world:

Give us this day, in memory and understanding and reverence of the love which our Lord Jesus Christ had for us and of those things which He said and did and suffered for us, our daily bread, your beloved Son, our Lord Jesus Christ.

Penetrating immediately to the profound meaning of this petition, Francis knows that the only bread which can satisfy our hunger is that which Christ gave us when He said: "I am the bread of life" (Jn 6:35). Francis asks the Father, who "draws" us to the Son (Jn 6:44), to give us that Bread.

We can partake of the Bread, the Father's beloved Son and our Lord Jesus Christ, "in memory and understanding and reverence of the love which our Lord Jesus Christ had for us." Christ's love gives us the strength to "make [ourselves] vulnerable to [our] enemies, both visible and invisible" (RegNB 16:11). It helps us to "preserve peace of mind and body" in all our trials (Adm 15:2) and to be on our guard against "the devil, [who] wishes to take from us the love of Jesus Christ" (RegNB 22:5).

When we realize that the Father has given us His beloved Son out of love for us and for the world, we see that life does have a meaning. Now we are completely convinced that Christ "loved [us] to the end" (Jn 13:1) because we are enlightened by "the true light, our Lord Jesus Christ" and have within us "the true wisdom of the Father" (2EpFid 66f.). Christ expressed this love during His earthly life by the "things which He said and did and suffered for us." Francis uses the phrase, "for us," twice to emphasize Christ's self-giving in love. We must remember this inexhaustible well of love, think about it, seize upon it, and understand it "with our whole mind" and especially hold it in "reverence."

That is how Francis introduces us to knowledge of the Son, who is the gift of the Father and the daily bread of those who put their trust in Him and abandon themselves to His loving care.

Christ in Francis's Writings

In general, accounts of Franciscan spirituality insist on the central role played in it by the humanity of Christ, especially the earthly aspects of His infancy, His preaching mission, and His Passion. These elements are certainly to be found in Francis's writings, but his view of Christ is wider and deeper than the usual assessments of his spirituality suggest.

The most striking thing about Francis's vision is, first, the omnipresence of God the Father and the rich texts which he devoted to it. The passages that speak explicitly about the Son are much fewer than those concerning the Father: there are two passages about the Son in the *Second Letter to the Faithful* (vv.3-15, 50-56), and, in the *Earlier Rule*, a combination of eight quotations from the New Testament describes Christ's presence in the heart of the community which He gathered around Him (RegNB 22:32-41). The *Letter to the Entire Order* deals more with the Eucharist than with Christ directly, and, similarly, Admonition 1 speaks more about spiritual knowledge of Him. It is especially in Christ's prayers, that is, in the fifteen psalms of the *Office of the Passion* and the three chains of quotations from chapter 17 of St. John's Gospel, that Francis looks into the depths of Christ's heart in a way that is far removed from a mere surface view of His humanity.

We must emphasize the fact that, when Francis speaks at any length about Christ, he always does so in the context of His Father or the Trinity (Adm 1; RegNB 22:41-55; 23:1-6; 2EpFid 3-14). In these texts, Francis lays particular stress on Christ's divinity. In certain passages (RegNB 22:27; 2EpFid 67; EpOrd 6,7,15,23-25), he begins by speaking about the Son and then, almost imperceptibly, changes to speaking about the mystery of God as God. For Francis, the Son is inseparable from the Father, and he never views Christ's humanity either in itself or as separate from His pre-existence in heaven or from His risen glory.

While Francis's treatment of the mystery of Christ is full and theologically accurate (see above, **Foundation: the Father Sends the Word,** p. 41), nevertheless he lays more stress on the Savior's teachings in the Gospel. In the *Earlier Rule* alone, he uses the phrase "The Lord says . . ." twenty-seven times (and ten times elsewhere), sometimes with the addition "in the Gospel" (six times). This phrase, "The Lord says . . . ," introduces Christ's words as they are found in the Synoptic Gospels, and this leads some authors to conclude that Francis knew only the Christ of the Synoptics. The quotations which Francis uses are not concerned with describing Christ but with conveying His instructions on how we should live and act.

In the next section, we shall examine the passages in Francis's writings which speak about Christ and in which he quotes from many different places in the Gospels. We shall try to discern how

Francis saw Christ's place in His Father's plan and described the ways that lead to the Father.

The Beloved Son in the Father's Plans

We have already briefly analyzed the two major passages from Francis's writings on the mystery of Christ. Here we shall endeavor to gather together and examine the other references to Christ in the writings.

Francis's christology, as contained in the *Earlier Rule* (RegNB 23:1-6) and the *Second Letter to the Faithful* (2EpFid 3-15), is rooted in the mystery of the Trinity. In the very act of creation, the Father has His Son by His side, since Father, Son, and Holy Spirit are "a perfect Trinity and simple Unity." Francis gives the Son titles which show that He is a Divine Person—"equal to the Father" (Adm 1:7); He is God (Adm 1:20; OffPass Ps 6:14); "Lord God of Israel" (OffPass Ps 6:15); "Lord of the universe, God and the Son of God" (EpOrd 27); "Son of the Most High, who is blessed forever" (EpOrd 4); "true God" (RegNB 23:3); "true Son of God" (Adm 1:8); "the Lord your God" (EpRect 8), and, finally, "The Word of the Father, so worthy, so holy and glorious" (2EpFid 4). If we gather together all the titles which Francis gives Christ in his writings, the total comes to forty-eight. The Son is eternally with the Father, knows what pleases Him, satisfies Him in everything, and alone is able to praise Him properly (RegNB 23:5). Yet He, like the Father, is worthy of being adored: "At the mention of [the Son's] name, you must adore Him with fear and reverence, prostrate on the ground" (EpOrd 4).

Like the Church's *Credo,* Francis places special emphasis on two cardinal points of Christ's human life—His coming into the world and His Passion—while making only brief references to other events in that life.

The Word, Creator along with the Father (RegNB 23:1,3; 2EpFid 12), was sent by the Father into the womb of the Virgin Mary to be born of her (2EpFid 4; OffPass Ps 15:3). In his vision of the Incarnation, Francis insists on the self-abnegation of the Son of glory. By taking on human flesh, Christ also took on part of our "frailty" (2EpFid 4), and His coming down "from the royal throne into the womb of the Virgin" (Adm 1:16) was a gesture of humility.

Because He was divine, He was "rich beyond all other things" (2EpFid 5; cf. 2Cor 8:9), yet He chose poverty in this world (2EpFid 5): "He was born along the way and placed in a manger since there was no room in the inn" (OffPass, Ps 15:7). Christ's "emptying Himself" in this manner did not consist simply in mere material poverty but rather in assuming the human condition, which was a much more radical form of poverty for Him.

In his writings, Francis mentions few details of Christ's life and ministry—His baptism (EpOrd 21), His fast in the wilderness (RegNB 3:11; RegB 3:6), His not being "ashamed" to be "a poor man and a transient [who] lived on alms" (RegNB 9:4f.), His coming "not . . . to be served but to serve" (Mt 20:28; Adm 4:1; RegNB 4:6) and, especially, His coming as the Good Shepherd, solicitous for His sheep and giving His life for them (mentioned four times—Adm 6:1; RegNB 22:32; 1EpFid 1:13; 2EpFid 56).

Francis summed up all Christ's earthly life, including the Incarnation and the Passion, in one simple formula that said everything for him: "the poverty and the humility and the holy Gospel of our Lord Jesus Christ" (RegB 12:4; RegNB 9:1; UltVol 1). While the events of Christ's life on earth do not occupy a prominent place in Francis's writings, the contents of our Lord's discourses, as found in the Synoptic Gospels as well as in St. John's Gospel, are quoted time and again with the introduction, "The Lord says . . ." or "The Lord commands . . ." (thirty-eight times).

But Francis treats at greatest length the events connected with our Lord's Passion: "As the Passion drew near, He celebrated the Passover with His disciples" (2EpFid 6). He relates the institution of the Eucharist with awed solemnity in the *Second Letter to the Faithful* (vv.6f.) and again in several other places (Adm 1:10; EpOrd 16; RegNB 20:6). He uses St. John's reference to the washing of the Apostles' feet (RegNB 6:4; Adm 5:2f.), as well as Christ's priestly prayer from the same Gospel (Jn 17). He tells of the events in Gethsemane—Christ's prayer, His sweating blood and His acceptance of His Father's will (2EpFid 8-11), His obedience unto death (EpOrd 46), and calling Judas the traitor "friend" (EpOrd 16; RegNB 22:2). Francis relates how Christ surrendered Himself willingly to His executioners (RegNB 22:2) and, finally, recalls "the cross and blood and death" of Christ (RegNB 23:3), His supreme sacrifice and self-immolation (2EpFid 11). In this way, he unfolds before our eyes the magnificent tapestry of the Passion of "the Son who is the Redeemer and Savior" (RegNB 16:7).

It was not for His own sake that Christ, "through whom all things were made," gave Himself up to death but to redeem us, to wash away our sins and save us (2EpFid 12f.; EpOrd 3). He did so because, as the Good Shepherd, He had willed to give His life for His sheep (RegNB 22:32; 1EpFid 1:13; 2EpFid 56; Adm 6:1) to show "the love which [He] had for us" (ExpPat 6). It is a striking fact that, contrary to the enthusiasm which medieval piety had for stark "realism" in recalling the details of the Passion—the scourging, the crowning with thorns, the spittle, the crucifixion— nothing of this appears in Francis's writings. The first six psalms of the *Office of the Passion* follow Christ, step by step, through His sufferings. But Francis does not indulge in a detailed, graphic description of those sufferings, nor does he dwell on our natural human reactions to the horrors of the Passion. Instead, he concentrates on revealing what was happening in the depths of Christ's heart by depicting Him as having a continued sorrowful but trusting "dialog" with His "most holy Father."

We may be surprised to find that Francis does not mention the Resurrection in his narrative of the Passion in chapter 23 of the *Earlier Rule*. Was this, perhaps, because he was influenced by the medieval tendency not to dwell on the Resurrection? Be that as it may, his references to Christ's glorious second coming show clearly that "[Christ] . . . is now not about to die, but . . . is eternally victorious and glorified" (EpOrd 22), while, in the *Office of the Passion*, three psalms (Ps 6,7,9) joyously celebrate the reality of the Resurrection. Of these psalms, the most remarkable is Ps 6, to be used at None of Good Friday, the time of Christ's death. In it, there is a heart-rending description of His descent into "the dust of death" and His "transfixion": "They have added grief to my wounds" (v.10). Then, without any pause or break, Francis bursts into the triumphant hymn of the Resurrected Christ: "I have slept and have risen and my most holy Father has received me with glory" (v.11). In the spirit of St. John's theology, the Crucified, "exalted on the earth," is shown to be triumphant even on the cross, and Francis depicts Him as exclaiming: "See, see that I am God, says the Lord." The psalms for Vespers on Good Friday (Ps 7) and for Matins on Easter Sunday (Ps 9) continue the Easter hymn of acclamation and thanksgiving by including all creation, and both psalms end by celebrating the Ascension. Thus Francis presents in full the *beata Passio*, "the blessed Passion," of Christ.

Christ's return in glory is also an important reason for Francis's giving thanks to the Father (RegNB 23:4). Christ appears here in His "majesty" as the judge at the end of time, welcoming into His kingdom those who have known, adored and served His Father, and sending into eternal fire those who have refused to be converted (cf. Mt 25:34). Francis announces this second coming three times in his psalms and exhorts us to be vigilant lest we be caught unawares (OffPass Ps 6:16; 7:11; 11:6; 22;27). The image of Christ as judge at the tribunal of justice (cf. Rom 14:10) appears frequently (five times) in his writings, depicted mostly, it is true, as calling upon souls to "render an account" (RegNB 4:6; 1EpFid 2:22; EpCler 14; EpRect 8) but also as promising rewards: "They will receive great honor before the tribunal of our Lord Jesus Christ" (RegNB 9:6).

So, Francis's christology is certainly in the "classical" tradition, for it contains the main elements of the Church's profession of faith. He adds no commentaries or elaborate speculations but contents himself with re-telling and contemplating the key events of salvation history. However, the amazing thing is that he, a "basic" Christian, without any formal theological training, was able to summon up a vision of such scope and depth.

Christ, Present with Us

Francis must have been particularly struck by our Lord's promise: "I am with you always, to the close of the age" (Mt 28:20) because he quotes it twice (Adm 1:22; RegNB 22:38). He saw it fulfilled in many ways—in Christ's living presence in the community but especially in His eucharistic presence and His presence in interceding for us:

> And let us have recourse to Him as to the shepherd and guardian of our souls, who says: I am the good shepherd who feeds my sheep and I lay down my life for my sheep (Jn 10:14f.). All of you are brothers. And do not call anyone on

earth your father, for one is your Father, the one in heaven. And do not let yourselves be called teachers, for your teacher is the one who is in heaven. If you remain in me, and my words remain in you, you may ask whatever you will and it will be done for you. Wherever two or three are gathered together in my name, I am there in the midst of them. The words which I have spoken to you are spirit and life. I am the way, the truth and the life.

This bouquet of texts from the *Earlier Rule* (RegNB 22:32-40) is made up of eight different quotations from the New Testament which the Church used during Lent and at Easter (four from St. John, three from St. Matthew and one from St. Peter). They were obviously not chosen at random but have a central unifying theme— the presence of Christ in the bosom of the Church.

From the first line onwards, Christ appears in the caring role of the Good Shepherd, the image preferred by Francis. He is "good," is concerned about His sheep, and sacrifices Himself for them. It is their having "recourse" to Him, their gathering around Him, that creates the community. This community of equals, of brothers, has only one teacher, Christ. They are called to "remain" in Him, to allow His words to dwell in them, with the assurance that their prayers will always be heard in the end. In particular, they can be certain that He is mysteriously present among them until the end of time because He is the very reason for their coming together. The community is sustained, prevented from stagnating, and renewed by the Gospel, His words, which are spirit and life. These words of Christ have the power to do this because they come from Him who is the way, the truth. and the life. Here Francis shows us what the Christian community is—he is thinking primarily about the friars—as well as how Christ is its one, true, ever-present center. This blending of scriptural quotations is one of the most beautiful of the passages which Francis devotes to Christ, and it has distinct overtones of tenderness.

"Honor the Lord in His words"

The first lines of the *Second Letter to the Faithful* speak about "the fragrant words of my Lord," perhaps an allusion to St. Paul's "the fragrance of the knowledge of (Christ)" (2Cor 2:14). Francis follows this immediately with a perspective that well deserves to be called theological. The words about which he is speaking come from a triple source. They are the words of the *Word*, who, in His turn, is the language of the *Father*. They are also the words of the *Holy Spirit* and are, therefore, spiritual and life-giving, that is, they are "spirit and life." The Father pronounced His eternal Word, who speaks in the Father's name, and His words, carried by the vital power of the Holy Spirit, bring life. Francis was so convinced and so awestruck that the Word was "spirit and life" (Jn 6:64), that he quotes this text four times (1EpFid 2:21; 2EpFid 2:3; RegNB 22:39; Test 13).

"The words" are so closely linked with Christ, the Word of God, that Francis almost sees them as one when it is a question of reading and interpreting Scripture, which he calls *divina littera*, "God's written word." Accordingly, he warns us that the study of Scripture must be done "in joy and gladness" (Adm 20:1), not, however, joy at knowing only the letter but at reaching the real meaning, which is given by God alone (Adm 7). On the other hand, as we shall see later, in most of the passages in his texts concerning the Eucharist, Francis insists on the word-sacrament link because "no one can be saved except through the holy words and Blood of our Lord Jesus Christ" (2EpFid 34).

The practical consequences of this spiritual knowledge of the Word of God will be the respect which is due to "His most holy names and written words" (Test 12). In the *Letter to the Entire Order* Francis recommends that "wherever [the brothers] come upon the written words of God, they [should] venerate them so far as they are able . . . , collect them and preserve them, thus honoring the Lord in the words which He spoke" (EpOrd 34-37; EpCler 12; 1EpCust 5).

"We . . . see . . . corporally . . . [the] Body and Blood"

In the *Letter to the Clergy* (EpCler 3), Francis wrote:

> In this world we have and see nothing corporally of the Most High except [His] Body and Blood, and the words through which we have been made and have been redeemed from death to life.

Here he unexpectedly presents us with a rich vision of the eucharistic mystery that has such an important place in his christology. He says: "In this world . . ." because the Risen Crucified Lord is no longer present to our senses, and the only signs of His presence that we can perceive "corporally" here and now are, first, the material elements, the "species," which support the sacramental mystery of His Body and Blood, and, second, "the words." These two inseparable realities, "the words" and Christ's gift of Himself in the Eucharist, are at the origin of our existence ("the words through which we have been made") and our salvation by the Passion ("and have been redeemed from death to life").

Although Francis never writes at length about "the most holy Body and most holy Blood" of Christ, he does speak about it in ten places in his writings, showing how important the Eucharist was to him. His references to the Eucharist are mostly just short reflections in passing, except in his *Letter to the Entire Order* and in Admonition 1. The circumstances which moved him to speak were varied. In the spirit of the movement launched by the Fourth Lateran Council and promoted by Pope Honorius III, he asks that due respect be paid to the Blessed Sacrament (EpCler; 1EpCust; EpRect). He insists that reverence is due to priests because they administer the Body and Blood of Christ (Adm 26; Test). He is also concerned about the worthy, frequent reception of the Eucharist (EpRect; 2EpFid; RegNB). Finally, in the *Letter to the Entire Order*, he deals with the conditions required for worthy, spiritual celebration of the Mass, while, in Admonition 1, he teaches the great importance of the Eucharist in the life of the Christian.

His scriptural quotations about the Eucharist refer to the institution (2EpFid 6:7; Adm 1:10), to chapter six of St. John's Gospel (v.54f.; Adm 1:11; RegNB 20:5; 2EpFid 23), and to St. Paul (1Cor 11:29), quotations that are especially important in the Church's theology of the Eucharist. The vocabulary he uses to describe the mystery is concrete and varied. The phrase, "Body and Blood" (twenty times), often accompanied by the adjectives "most holy" (twelve times), is the one that occurs most frequently, while St. John's expression "flesh and blood" is not overlooked (used three times). As general terms to designate the liturgical action, he has "sacrifice" (three times), "sacrament" (twice), "Mass" (twice), "celebration" (once), as well as "mystery" (or "ministry"? twice). The verbs "to sanctify" (five times), "to sacrifice" (three times), "to confect" (*conficere*, once) emphasize the dynamic nature of the celebration. When speaking about communion, he refers to "administering" (by the priests) and "receiving" (*recipere*, fourteen times; *sumere*, six times). In addition, he gives details of the liturgical action and describes

> the sacrament [of the Body of Christ], which is sanctified by the words of the Lord upon the altar at the hands of the priest in the form of bread and wine (Adm 1:9).

Everything is there—the altar, the bread and wine, the words of consecration "at the hands of the priest," hands which Francis also mentions elsewhere (EpCler 8; EpOrd 22:26; Adm 1:18), as well as "the chalices, the corporals and the altar-linens upon which the Body and Blood of our Lord are sacrificed" (EpCler 4), and other liturgical objects (EpOrd 34).

The inner reality of the sacrament is bound up with "the word." In five places, when Francis is speaking about the Body and Blood, he explicitly states that "it cannot become His Body without first being consecrated by [His] word" (EpCler 2) and that "in the power of the words of Christ the sacrament of the altar is celebrated" (EpOrd 37 and again in 1EpCust 2; Adm 1:9; 2EpFid 34). He also makes the connection between "word" and the Eucharist in two other passages (Test 10-12; EpCler 11f.). In this mystery, "the Lord of the universe, God and the Son of God . . . hides Himself under the little form of bread" (EpOrd 27). Christ's presence is not static, however, for, according to the *Second Letter to the Faithful* (2EpFid 2-15), the Eucharist is the memorial of the Passover, the Passion and the victory over death which Christ experienced in His difficult but total surrender to the Father's will. It was for us and to us that "He . . . [gave] Himself totally" (EpOrd 29), and the Father "wills that all of us should be saved through Him and be saved by Him" (2EpFid 12-14). Francis applies to the Eucharist a passage inspired by St. Paul (Col 1:20): "Our Lord Jesus . . . , in whom that which is in the heavens and on the earth is brought to peace and is reconciled to the all-powerful God" (EpOrd 13). In this way, Francis extends to the Eucharist the biblical text which refers to Christ's saving death as "making peace by the blood of the cross." That is to say, the Eucharist brings unity and peace to the whole universe. While Francis holds up the Eucharist as a vision of reconciliation and peace, with the living, glorious God at the center, he also views it paradoxically as a descent, a self-abasement, in which we see God's humility. He describes this forcefully in the *Letter to the Entire Order* (EpOrd 27f.) and in *Admonition* 1 (16-18):

> O admirable heights and sublime lowliness! O sublime humility! O humble sublimity! That the Lord of the universe, God and the Son of God, so humbles Himself that for our salvation He hides Himself under the little form of bread! See, daily He humbles Himself as when He came from the royal throne into the womb of the Virgin; daily He comes to us in a humble form; daily He comes down from the bosom of the Father upon the altar in the hands of the priest.

The startling contrast is between the "sublimity," the awesome dignity, of the Lord of the universe, who is God and the Son of God, and His insignificant presence in the very ordinary, everyday bread in which He is given to us. He "hides" His true glory from all our senses. God's humility is not a gesture of humiliation; instead, He is presenting Himself incognito, hidden. Admonition 1 sees this humility as a kind of continuation of the Incarnation. For God, becoming human meant "leav[ing] His royal throne" to take on human anonymity, and every day He wishes to go even further—or lower. God no longer appears to us in human form but as a morsel of bread, "under the little form of bread." In speaking about humility in the Eucharist, Francis was not merely referring to different degrees of humility but to the profound theological mystery of God's appearance in the world in a new form. In His Incarnation and then in His eucharistic presence, the Son showed His own humility first but also that of the Father who accepted the descent of His only Son "from [His] bosom . . . upon the altar at the hands of the priest" (Adm 1:18).

No doubt because of the contemporary anti-sacramental movements, Francis emphasized the role of the priest-celebrant to the exclusion of everyone else: "[The priests] alone must administer [the

Eucharist] and not others" (2EpFid 35; Adm 26:3; Test 10). This is the reason he gives for the respect due to priests. Yet in the *Letter to the Entire Order*, he states that it is "the most high Lord . . . alone [who] does these things as He pleases" (EpOrd 15), and not only He but also "the Lord God the Father and . . . the Holy Spirit, the Paraclete" (EpOrd 33). The same letter urges "that only one Mass . . . be celebrated each day in the places in which the brothers stay" and that the other priest-friars should be content "to assist at the celebration of the other priest" (EpOrd 30f.) because "our Lord Jesus Christ fills those who are present and absent . . . . Although He may seem to be present in many places, He nonetheless remains indivisible" (EpOrd 33). This could be taken to imply that Francis is lessening the importance of the Mass and the Eucharist. Yet the Mass remains for him the ultimate reality, the sole means of bringing us Christ in the Eucharist. However, beyond providing us with this presence, the supreme aim of the Mass and the Eucharist is to demonstrate and acknowledge Christ's love for us (ExpPat 6). There is nothing surprising in this since Francis, following St. Paul (1Cor 11:27-29), frequently insists on the need for the "discernment" required for the worthy reception of the Eucharist (six times—1EpFid 1:3; 2:2; 2EpFid 22-24,63; EpOrd 17-19; Adm 1:12f.; RegNB 20:5; EpCler 6).

We can now see more clearly the place of the Eucharist in Francis's christology. The Eucharist is the special, perceptible, "corporal" sign of Christ's presence here and now in the Church and the world. "In this way, the Lord is always with His faithful" (Adm 1:22) as a material sign that condenses and sums up the whole mystery of Christ in the context of the Trinity. At the same time, the Eucharist is a veil which we can penetrate only with the help of the Holy Spirit.

There is, however, a limitation to this view. Francis does not present the ecclesial dimension of the Eucharist as the total Body of Christ, except possibly in the *Letter to the Entire Order*, where he speaks about the community celebration of the Mass (EpOrd 30-33).

"He humbled Himself to ask His Father for us"

In his writings, Francis prays to God and praises Him but, in addition, many of the prayers he composed are Christ's prayers to the Father. Such prayers start from Christ's pain-filled prayer of acceptance in Gethsemane (2EpFid 8-10), which Francis enlarges upon and expands in the fifteen psalms of his *Office of the Passion*. In these psalms, Francis depicts Christ as praying to His Father twelve times, the other three being Te Deums for victory chanted by the Church *(vox Ecclesiae).* Francis's psalter, which portrays the Son as praying, is not, properly speaking, a prayer of intercession for humanity but is, rather, a meditation which the suffering yet victorious Son makes in the presence of His Father. Francis gives us this meditation as a model for the attitude we should have in suffering and in the joy of salvation. Here the Son is teaching us how we should act before the Father as long as we live.

But Christ also intercedes for us. Francis presents Christ's prayers for us by quoting seventeen of the twenty-six verses of chapter 17 of St. John's Gospel (RegNB 22:41-55). He introduces this passage solemnly by marveling at the fact that the Son "who laid down His life for His sheep" (2EpFid 56), "humbled Himself to ask His Father for us and to make His name known to us" (RegNB 22:41). Yet Christ's prayer here is not primarily concerned with us but with the glory of His Father (vv.41,42,54) and of the Son (v.41). However, it does apply to and encompass all humanity. The Son asks that we be protected in the name of the Father, that we be "one" (v.45), and "have joy within [us]" (v.46). He prays that we be "protect[ed] from evil" (v.48), "sanctified in truth" (v.52), and "be completely one" (v.53). He wants us to know that the Son has been sent by the Father (v.53) and especially that we are loved by Christ as He loves His own Father (vv.53f.). His pleads that the love with which the Father loves Christ may be in us (v.54), and that we may be where Christ is (v.55) in order to see the Father's glory in His kingdom (v.55).

We should note that, in this prayer, Francis has retained all the petitions concerning the disciples. We are assured that the Lord is present under the humble appearances of bread and wine and is living and active in His words at the heart of the community which His love unto death has brought together. But Christ also

stands before His Father unceasingly interceding for us, His
brothers and sisters, until we can join Him where He is—in the
kingdom of the Father. There, He and the Holy Spirit will sing
the eternal hymn of thanksgiving for everything the Father has
willed to accomplish (RegNB 23:5).

In the Footsteps of Christ

But how are we to discover the living Lord, the way to the Father,
behind the words and material signs? The humanity of Christ as
His contemporaries knew it no longer exists, and, even if it did, our
purely sense knowledge of it, our merely seeing it with our eyes,
would be of little benefit. Two of Francis's texts address this
point—Admonition 1 and the *First* and *Second Letters to the
Faithful*.

"[To] see and believe according to the Spirit and the Godhead"

The first Admonition, brief as it is, could be entitled "A short
treatise on knowledge of the Father and the Son." It is divided into
three parts: the first speaks about the Father in the Trinity (vv.1-
7); the second looks at the Lord Jesus, first as He appears in history
and then in His sacramental presence (vv.8-13); the third is an
exhortation which repeats the terms relating to Christ's presence
in history and in the Eucharist (vv.14-22).

The Father lives in inaccessible light (1Tim 6:16). He is spirit
(Jn 4:24), and no one has ever seen Him (Jn 1:18), because that is
possible only in the Spirit who gives life (Jn 6:64). Only the Son,
who is the way, the truth, and the life, can lead us to Him. To
know the Son is to know the Father also: one who sees the Son sees
the Father (Jn 14:6-9; Adm 1:1-5). This accumulation of texts
hammers home the point that the Father is inaccessible and that
the Son is the only way to reach Him.

It all seems so simple—if we want to see the Father, we must do
so with the Son. However, notice that Francis adds: "But neither,
inasmuch as He is equal to the Father, is the Son seen by anyone
other than the Father [or] other than the Holy Spirit" (v.7). This
only increases our difficulty and leaves us where we started. The
Son, who is our way to knowing the Father, is Himself unknowable

by the very fact that He is the Son of God. To solve this dilemma, Francis next ponders the way to gain access to the mystery of Christ. He reflects on the twofold presence of Christ, historical and sacramental. The Christ of history was seen by His contemporaries "according to His humanity" (v.8) and in "true flesh" (vv.19f.). But He was also "the true Son of God" (v.8), who could be seen only with the eyes of faith. It is the same with the Eucharist. The bread and wine and the sacramental rite are there, perceptible by the senses (vv.9,19,21), but in reality the bread and wine are "the most holy Body and Blood of our Lord Jesus Christ, . . . living and true" (vv.9,21). Our knowledge of Christ in this double state is likewise double, derived as it is from our "bodily eyes" (*intuitus carnis*, v.21) and our "eyes of faith" (*oculi spirituales*, v.20).

When Francis is speaking about knowledge "according to the flesh," he uses the verb "to see" alone (vv.8f.,20f.), but when he is referring to total, spiritual knowledge, he says "to see and believe" (vv.8f.,20f.). In the first case, even the Apostles were able to see only the "flesh" (v.20), that is, Christ's humanity alone (v.8); and we, today, can see only the sacramental ritual and species. But if we, like the Apostles, begin to "see and believe according to the Spirit and the Godhead" (vv.8f.), contemplating the Eucharist with the eyes of faith, then we shall attain to true knowledge of Christ, both in His earthly life and in His sacramental presence. But such knowledge comes from the Spirit of the Lord, the Holy Spirit, who alone makes it possible:

> Therefore it is the Spirit of the Lord, who lives in His faithful, who receives the most holy Body and Blood of the Lord. All others who do not share in this same Spirit and who presume to receive Him eat and drink judgment to themselves (Adm 1:12f.).

In this way, a path of knowledge towards the mystery of the Trinity is opened up for us. We begin with what we can see and grasp of Christ—His humanity, His flesh, and the sacrament. However, we must not be satisfied with this surface knowledge but must allow ourselves to be inhabited by the Spirit, who will open our spiritual eyes. Then we can be introduced to the inner life of Christ "according to the Spirit and the Godhead." It is He, through His divine and human natures, who will show us the face of the invisible Father. The path of knowledge of Christ leads, in the Spirit, to the depths of the Father.

"Spouses, brothers and mothers of our Lord Jesus Christ"

Francis's two *Letters to the faithful* describe what awaits those who have persevered in fidelity to the Gospel. "The Spirit of the Lord will rest upon them, and He will make His home and dwelling among them" (1EpFid 1:5; 2EpFid 48). This resting and dwelling of the Spirit in the hearts of the faithful will make them enter into communion with the Father and the Son:

> They will be children of the heavenly Father, whose works they do. And they are spouses, brothers and mothers of our Lord Jesus Christ. We are spouses when the faithful soul is joined to Jesus Christ by the Holy Spirit. We are brothers when we do the will of His Father who is in heaven. We are mothers when we carry Him in our hearts and bodies through love and a pure and sincere conscience; we give birth to Him through His holy manner of working, which should shine before others as an example (2EpFid 49-53).

In addition to asserting that we are children of the Father, Francis joyfully describes the bond which the Spirit establishes with the Son by repeating and developing three images from the New Testament—Christ the spouse (Jn 3:29; Mk 2:19) and Christ the son and brother (Mk 3:34f.). The espousals of the faithful soul (feminine) with Christ, through the working of the Holy Spirit, make us spouses (masculine), a graceful way of combining masculine and feminine by using the masculine form of the world "spouse."

Being brothers of Christ brings us into a relationship with the Father. Our motherhood of Christ, a theme which the Fathers, from Origen and Ambrose onwards, have commented upon, is described in metaphorical and realistic terms as pregnancy and giving birth. We shall return to this point later when we deal with Francis's views on humanity. It will be enough here to allow Francis to show his joy at our closeness to Christ:

Oh, how glorious it is, how holy, consoling, beautiful and wondrous it is to have a Father in heaven! Oh, how holy, consoling, beautiful and wondrous it is to have a Spouse! Oh, how holy and how loving, pleasing, humble, peaceful, sweet, lovable and desirable above all things to have such a Brother and Son who laid down His life for His sheep and who prayed to the Father for us! (2EpFid 54-56).

This is the only place where Francis gives free rein to his unbounded joy by using the frequent exclamation "Oh!" and the many adjectives which express his keen delight—"holy," "consoling," "beautiful," "wondrous," "sweet," "lovable," "desirable." It is true that, when speaking elsewhere about the Father, he also uses an abundance of similar adjectives (RegNB 23:9-11; LaudDei; ExpPat 2,4), but he does so with a kind of reverent restraint, whereas here we can sense a freer, more personal reaction of joy and pleasure.

Praying to Christ

While almost all of Francis's twenty prayers are addressed to God the Father, he directs to Christ only one ancient prayer taken from the Feast of the Holy Cross:

We adore you, Lord Jesus Christ, in all your churches throughout the world, and we bless you, for through your holy cross you have redeemed the world (Test 5).

This is not a prayer of petition but of praise, and the adoration which he expresses here appears again more explicitly in the opening of his *Letter to the Entire Order*:

Greetings in Him who redeemed us and washed us in His most precious blood. At the mention of His name, you must adore Him with fear and reverence, prostrate on the ground. It is the name of our Lord Jesus Christ, the name of that Son of the Most High, who is blessed forever (EpOrd 3f.).

Here Francis is speaking about the greatness of the Lord of glory and His work of salvation for us, and he invites his brothers to prostrate themselves in adoration before His majesty. Even if Francis had addressed his *Prayer before the Crucifix* to Christ—and this does not seem to have been the case—he called the One whom he invoked there "Most High" and "glorious," a Being of light and beneficence ("enlighten the darkness of my heart"; "give me"). In his *Praises to be Said at All the Hours*, after the threefold praise and acclamation of God, he greeted Christ in the words of the Book of Revelation (5:12):

> The Lamb who was slain is worthy to receive power and divinity and wisdom and strength and honor and glory and blessing.

And he closes with the resounding invitatory in which he obviously addresses the Son in the first phrase but then changes, almost imperceptibly, to praise God in all His glory:

> Let every creature in heaven, on earth, in the sea and in the depths, give praise, glory, honor and blessing to Him who suffered so much for us, who has given so many good things, and who will continue to do so for the future. For He is our power and strength, He who alone is good, who is most high, who is all-powerful, admirable and glorious; who alone is holy, praiseworthy and blessed throughout endless ages. Amen (2EpFid 61f.).

Francis did not view Christ in His humanity alone. Without separating the human from the divine in Christ, Francis saw Him in His present-day mysterious actuality, no longer dead but living, no longer flesh but Spirit. It is He "in whose footsteps we must follow" (2EpFid 13; RegNB 1:1; 22:2; EpOrd 51; EpLeo 3) and whose "words, . . . life, . . . teaching and . . . Holy Gospel we must cling to" (RegNB 22:41). "And in this way the Lord is always with His faithful" (Adm 1:22).

"The Spirit of the Lord and Its Holy Manner of Working"

In Francis's major writings, when he speaks in general about God the Father and His works, he always shows the Spirit present with and beside the Son (RegNB 21:1-6; 2EpFid 3:48-51; Adm 1).

He uses the word *Spiritus* seventy-three times, mostly to designate the Holy Spirit (forty times) or at least a divine power or force (twenty-four times). On other occasions, he applies the word to the human spirit (five times) or to invisible spirits, either good (once) or bad (three times). When he mentions the Holy Spirit, he mostly does so as part of an explicitly trinitarian formula, either liturgical (ten times) or otherwise (eleven times).

In his writings, Francis has whole lists of the attributes of the Father and the Son, but he gives the Holy Spirit only three classical names. Most often he says "the Holy Spirit"; but he also uses "the Paraclete" (RegNB 23:5f.; EpOrd 33; SalBMV 2; Test 40) and "the Spirit of the Lord" (Adm 1:12; 12:1; RegNB 17:14; RegB 10:8; 1EpFid 1:6; 2EpFid 48). It seems that he reserved no particular attribute for the Holy Spirit but was content to call Him the "Holy" One or the Paraclete-Consoler (he applies the title "Consoler" once, but to the Father in ExpPat 1) or "the Spirit of the Lord" to indicate either His place in the Trinity or His relationship with the Lord (Father or Son?).

He uses the word *paraclitum* as an adjective in the sense of "consoling," "reassuring," when he is singing about the joy of those upon whom the Spirit of the Lord rests (2EpFid 55). He may be referring to the Spirit when he uses the striking expression: "your holy love with which you have loved us" (RegNB 23:3), which comes immediately after his mentioning the Son as Co-creator. And he may again be thinking of the mysterious figure of the ineffable Spirit when he attributes to God certain qualities which imply that He is vulnerable and tender, that is, when he says that God is "merciful," "gentle," "delectable," "sweet," "lovable," and "totally desirable above all else."

"Its holy manner of working"

Francis often associates the Holy Spirit with the Father and the Son (twenty-one times) and shows that the Spirit, like the other Divine Persons, is always at work. In fact, it was "through [His] only Son with the Holy Spirit . . . [that the Father] created all things spiritual and material" (RegNB 23:1). Francis asks the Paraclete, with the Son, to be the principal singer of the hymn of thanksgiving which he addresses to the Father (RegNB 23:5f.).

The Spirit lives in the faithful (Rom 8:9; Adm 1:12) and makes their "members . . . temples of the Holy Spirit" (1Cor 6:19; RegNB 12:6). As the Spirit of adoration, He gives the faithful the power "to worship Him in spirit and in truth" (Jn 4:23f.—quoted twice; RegNB 22:31; 2EpFid 19:20) and allows them to share, as far as they can, in His own life in the Trinity as the reciprocal love of the Father and the Son.

Moreover, Francis rightly calls Him "the Spirit of holy prayer and devotion to which all other things of our earthly existence should contribute" (RegB 5:2). It is also He who is "spirit and life" (Jn 6:64, quoted four times—RegNB 22:39; 1EpFid 2:21; 2EpFid 3; Test 13), who gives vitality and efficacy to the word of God and without whom that word would be empty, "the letter [that] kills" (2Cor 3:6; Adm 7:1). The words of the Gospel which Francis wishes to proclaim are "the words of the Holy Spirit, which [therefore] are spirit and life" (2EpFid 3). Revealing the inexhaustible meanings of the word of God, the Spirit helps us to understand the very core of that word, to know and acknowledge the divinity of Christ: "No one can say 'Jesus is Lord' except in the Holy Spirit" (1Cor 12:3; Adm 8:1). He is, therefore, the true interpreter of Sacred Scripture, and when He imparts knowledge of the Scriptures, He leads the recipient to give thanks "to the most High Lord God" (Adm 7:4). He is active with the Father and the Son in the consecration of the Eucharist (EpOrd 33), and it is He

> . . . who lives in His faithful, who receives the most holy Body and Blood of the Lord. All [those] who do not share in this same Spirit and who presume to receive Him, eat and drink judgment to themselves (Adm 1;12f.).

The Holy Spirit is the only door through which we can gain access to the inaccessible light in which the invisible Father lives, and the path that leads there is the humanity of the Son and His sacrament seen "according to the Spirit and the Godhead," for it is the Spirit who give us "the eyes of faith" to "contemplate" Christ in the Eucharist (Adm 1:20; the only time Francis uses the verb "to contemplate").

In Francis's concise account of the soul's spiritual journey (EpOrd 50-52), the Spirit prepares us to follow in the Son's footsteps and to come to the Most High Father. The Spirit cleanses, enlightens, and finally sets on fire the innermost recesses of our souls, and His grace and light foster "all [the] holy virtues" in our hearts, changing us from being "faithless" into being "faithful to God" (SalBMV 6). It is in His love, "the charity of the Spirit" (Gal 5:13, after the Vulgate) that He shows us God's love for us (cf. Rom 5:5), the love which inspires the friars to "serve and obey one another" (RegNB 5:14).

Francis's two *Rules* contain two passages which summarize in a few lines his understanding of the Spirit's action in the life of his brothers. There he uses the expression, "the Spirit of the Lord" (RegNB 17:14-16; RegB 10:8-10). What actions, movements or attitudes awaken the presence of the Spirit in the brothers' hearts?

> The Spirit of the Lord wishes the flesh to be mortified and despised, [deemed] worthless and rejected. And it strives for humility and patience and the pure and simple and true peace of the spiritual person. And above all things, it always longs for the divine fear and the divine wisdom and the divine love of the Father and of the Son and of the Holy Spirit (RegNB 17:14-16).

Strictly speaking, "the Spirit of the Lord" which Francis contrasts with "the spirit of the flesh" in the preceding verses (vv.11-13) can only be an attitude of the soul itself, inspired by the power of God. But elsewhere in his writings, Francis always uses the title "the Spirit of the Lord" to mean the Person of the Holy Spirit (Adm 1:12; 12:1; 1EpFid 1:6; 2EpFid 48; RegB 10:8), and that leads us to conclude that here, too, he is speaking about the Holy Spirit Himself.

According to Francis, the first effect of that Spirit is to make us aware of the "fleshly" defects within us, our selfishness, our lack of openness, and our self-sufficiency, which shut out God and neighbor. These defects must "be mortified and despised, [deemed] worthless and rejected," to quote Francis's own words. It is true that the terms he uses here are very negative ones, but they were common in an ascetical tradition that is not without ambiguity.

In contrast, the Spirit wishes to awaken in us the basic Christian values: humility (self-knowledge, self-acceptance); patience (perseverance, endurance, long-suffering); simplicity (a heart emptied of self and centered on God and His promises); true peace of mind (an interior calm, solidly founded on hope). When we have rejected evil and have chosen to follow the path of truth about ourselves, the Spirit can begin to teach us how to perfect the work we have begun. He wishes "the flesh" to die in us and sets about creating appropriate attitudes; but, above all, He wants to awaken in our hearts the ardent *desire* ("He yearns jealously . . ." [cf. Jas 4:5]) for the fear and reverence, the savor and taste of love, which union with the Father, Son, and Spirit gives.

The following text has the same structure as the two passages from the *Rules*. Here Francis puts us on our guard against negative behavior, "the spirit of the flesh"—pride, vainglory, envy, avarice, anxiety, criticism, an ambitious desire for knowledge— and he insists that the brothers instead

> pursue what they must desire above all things: to have the Spirit of the Lord and His holy manner of working, to pray always to Him with a pure heart and to have humility, patience in persecution and weakness and to love those who persecute us, find fault with us, or rebuke us, because the Lord says: Love your enemies, and pray for those who persecute and slander you. Blessed are those who suffer persecution for the sake of justice, for theirs is the kingdom of heaven. But whoever perseveres to the end, he will be saved (RegB 10:8-10).

God is desirable, and Francis emphasizes desire for Him some eight times in his writings. In this instance, the Spirit Himself is desired, and the first fruit of His presence is the prayer of a pure heart. Then, as we have said, come humility and patience. Finally, we reach the apparently paradoxical climax, love of enemies, which undoubtedly best demonstrates the unconditional love which God has for us sinners.

"The Spirit of the Lord will rest on them"

There are passages in Francis's writings which invite us to penetrate deeper and learn more about the power of the Spirit, His activity in us, and the personal bond that He forges with each one of us believers. We must desire "to have the Spirit of the Lord" because "He lives in His faithful" (Adm 1:12), "rests on them" as He did on the Davidic Messiah (Is 11:2) and on Christ at His baptism (Jn 1:32), and He "will make His home and dwelling among them" (cf. Jn 14:23; Eph 2:22; 1EpFid 1:6; 2EpFid 48; cf. RegNB 22:37).

Francis is making here an original, personal transference of emphasis. As he sees it, the indwelling of the Holy Spirit, as described in John 14:23 and in the *Earlier Rule* (22:27)—"We will come to him and make our home with him"—is not primarily the work of the Father and the Son but is the result of the Spirit's own coming and resting in our souls: "The Spirit of the Lord will rest [upon them] and He will make His home and dwelling among them" (2EpFid 48). The effect of the Spirit's presence is to bring the faithful soul into a relationship with the Father and the Son.

When Francis describes this new relationship—the bond of sonship with the Father and the triple bond of spouse, brother and mother with Christ—he makes the role of the Spirit quite clear when he says: "We are spouses when the faithful soul is joined (*conjungitur*: "by a conjugal bond") to Jesus Christ by the Holy Spirit" (2EpFid 51). This conjugal union between "the faithful soul" and Christ is contracted and consummated by means of a mysterious intervention of the Spirit, the nature of which Francis does not explain further. We see only that Francis regarded the Spirit's role as initiating and sealing the marriage since He is "Love," which is precisely the name of the Holy Spirit's role as prime Revealer of God's love for us (Rom 5:5).

This special insight may perhaps explain the daring formula which Francis originated when he gave Mary the title of "the spouse of the Holy Spirit" (AntOffPass). He did not hesitate to give the same title also to the Poor Ladies of St. Clare: "[You] have taken the Holy Spirit as your spouse" (FormViv 1). Almost all Christian spiritual tradition has regarded Christ as the bridegroom and the soul as the bride. Francis knew this tradition and repeated it, as we have seen. But he brought something new and unusual to it by speaking about the marriage between the soul and the Holy Spirit. He thus opened the way for another theological approach that has so far been very little used.

Scripture tells us that the Spirit descended upon and "over-shadowed" Mary (cf. Lk 1:35). To this image Francis adds that she was dedicated and "consecrated" by "the Spirit the Paraclete" at the solemn celebration of "the most holy Father in heaven . . . with His most holy beloved Son" (SalBMV 2). Was it this perhaps that inspired Francis to call Mary "the spouse of the Holy Spirit"?

"Spiritual, . . . spiritually"

When we consider the presence and action of the Holy Spirit in this way, we understand better the weight of meaning in Francis's words "spiritual" (*spiritualis*, which he uses nine times in the original Latin) and "spiritually" (*spiritualiter*—eight times), especially in the older parts of his *Rules*. In fact, seven of the eight times he employs *"spiritualiter"* occur in his *Rules*, while the adjective, *"spiritualis,"* is present in them six out of the total nine times he uses this term. He refers to seeing with spiritual eyes (*"cum oculis spiritualibus"* [Adm 1:20]) or, in Armstrong-Brady's translation, "with the eyes of faith"; "spiritual wisdom" (2EpFid 67); "spiritual desire" (RegNB 2:11); "spiritual advice" (RegNB 12:3f.); "spiritual friends" (RegB 4:2); a friar's "spiritual" brother (*"fratrem suum spiritualem"* [RegB 6:8]) or, in Armstrong-Brady, his "brother according to the spirit." The relationships between the friars must be lived "spiritually" (*spiritualiter* [RegNB 4:2; 5:8]) or, in Armstrong-Brady, "according to the spirit" (RegNB 5:4f.) and "wholeheartedly" (RegNB 7:15). Francis uses the same term, "spiritually" (*spiritualiter*), to describe behavior. This is a way of applying the Gospel teachings (RegNB 2:4), of living among nonbelievers (RegNB 16:5), of observing the *Rule* (RegB 10:4). We are to judge such activities by the "spiritual" way we perform them. In the last analysis, it is always the Spirit who makes it possible for one to live and act "spiritually," who dwells within and leads the Christian person.

At first glance, the Holy Spirit may seem to play only a modest part in Francis's writings since he mentions the Spirit rarely and only under a few different titles. Yet, on closer examination, we see that, while the Spirit's presence in the writings is unobtrusive, it is all-pervasive. As the Byzantine liturgy proclaims, He is truly "the Spirit of the Lord everywhere present." Although the Holy

Spirit's face is hidden from us, Francis often describes His activity in the soul, His "holy manner of working." Francis warns us that we can "insult" (EpOrd 18; cf. Heb 10:29 "outrage") or even "extinguish" (RegB 5:2) "the Spirit of the Lord." We are told that the Spirit's presence or absence is shown by our behavior (Adm 12), that He is always at work where the Father and the Son are (EpOrd 33), and that, with the Son, He showers blessings on those who live in this world according to the Gospel (Test 40). However, while Francis speaks clearly about the role of the Spirit in relation to individual souls, he does not touch upon the Spirit's activity in the Church as a whole. In this respect, he adopts the approach of St. John the Evangelist rather than that of St. Luke in the Acts of the Apostles.

Francis's "Theology"

The summary we have just given demonstrates the wealth of doctrine to be found in even a few pages of Francis's writings composed in differing circumstances. Although he was a medieval layman with no formal theological training and expressed himself only in fragments scattered throughout his writings, he displayed an astonishingly comprehensive knowledge of the mystery of the Trinity. His theological thoughts on God followed the pattern of the Church's *Credo*—and there was nothing original about that. What was original was the way he assimilated this *Credo* and made it his own. Besides, while the substance of his hymn of thanksgiving and praise to the Trinity (cf. RegNB 23:1-6) was that of the Creed, he added other elements, especially his insistence on the Triune God's concern with us humans whom God never ceases to shape in His own image.

Without undue exaggeration, we could say that Francis's theological vision reflects the scope, the hierarchy of values, and the balance of the New Testament's biblical revelations. His writings contain all the essentials of Christian teaching on God, since in them we find St. John the Evangelist's insights into the relationship between the Father and the Son, a full account of our Lord's preaching as recorded in the Synoptic Gospels, and some of St. Paul's traits which Francis developed greatly when dealing with human conduct and attitudes.

We should also note Francis's "hierarchy of values" or, rather, "his hierarchy of Persons." Authors are continually writing about his apparent preoccupation with the humanity of Christ and making it the center of his spirituality to the exclusion of everything else. But his writings demonstrate that his teaching is actually centered on the Father, who holds the primacy in everything. Within the mystery of the Trinity, there is an order of relationships, a *taxis* ("arrangement," in Greek), which he grasped and wrote about without using technical theological terminology.

This primacy or "monarchy" of the Father in Francis's writings does not suppress or diminish in the slightest the Son's divinity or humanity or the Paraclete's presence and "manner of working." Instead, Francis saw that the relationships in the Trinity make for harmony and balance. Moreover, our investigation into his theology shows that he paid special attention to the nature and role of each Person of the Trinity, if we are to judge by the number of pages he devoted to each. He deals at greatest length with the Son's nature and work because Christ appeared in history and is therefore more accessible to us, while the invisible Father, although central, and the "inaccessible" Holy Spirit are less within the reach of our minds and language.

Although Francis's teaching as found in his writings is rich and balanced, it is not a theology in the usual sense of the term. He does not start from a defined philosophical base and go on to speculate and develop ideas or theories. With the exception of those two unusual passages (RegNB 23:1-6; 2EpFid 2-15), Francis does not attempt to give a comprehensive summation of his doctrine. He simply announces and proclaims his belief in what he had learned about the faith from the liturgy and had come to know interiorly through the enlightenment of Him who is "Spirit and Life." The knowledge he received through learning and enlightenment was personal to him, as we can see from the choices he made from the broad range of the Christian heritage, choices which omitted nothing important. In addition, there are his spiritual experiences, to which he never explicitly refers but which we can sense in the awed adoration and intense joy that suffuse his writings.

In the long list of Christian theological and spiritual authors, Francis is unusual and difficult to classify. While his thought is close to that of the Desert Fathers, especially in his vision of us humans and our spiritual journey, his theological scope is wider than theirs, with the exception of Evagrius. He is not a profound theologian, like the Fathers of the Church, although some of his writings resemble their homilies; nor is he a mystical writer, like Tauler or St. John of the Cross. Instead, his "theology" is a "Gospel" theology in the sense that he absorbs and retells the Gospels and rejoices in the revealed word of God but without taking anything away from it or adding too much of his own to it.

Although his writings are easily accessible because his language is simple and redolent of Scripture, the thoughts and views they present still need to be interpreted for the modern world, as indeed is the case with all older texts. We have done some of this interpretation and updating in the previous pages, and we shall continue this work in greater detail at the end of this study, although we are aware that this task really belongs to the reader.

Chapter 4

Humanity, a Vision of Contrasts

Francis addresses his song of thanksgiving to the Father in particular (RegNB 23:1-6), yet we humans and the creation of which we are a part also figure there prominently. His hymn of thankful praise to God celebrates us, too, since God and we are inseparable and, in a way, interdependent.

So far, we have been considering the mystery of God as revealed and proclaimed so eloquently by Francis, and we come next to his "anthropology," his thoughts about humanity, about people. Once again, we shall begin with the two passages which we took above as models and guidelines (RegNB 23:1-6; 2EpFid 2-15). We shall try to describe as completely as possible the vision in contrasts which Francis had of each one of us, for we are a combination of greatness and wretchedness. We shall also reflect on the Church as the collective aspect of that vision.

Creation, God's Loving Plan

Before turning his thoughts to us, Francis fixes his attention on God, whose power, "otherness," majesty, Lordship and Fatherhood he celebrates, as if to imply that we can be truly known only in relation to God and that whatever dignity we may possess is founded on, and guaranteed by, Him. Moreover, Francis expresses his thoughts on the relationship between God and us in the form of a hymn of thanksgiving. In fact, for him, "giving thanks" seems to be a basic necessity, for he uses that phrase four times in the first verses of his prayer (RegNB 23:1-6). "Giving thanks" presupposes that we first receive and acknowledge God's "grace," His free gift, without hoarding it or attributing it to ourselves but returning it to God:

> And let us refer all good to the most high and supreme Lord
> God, and acknowledge that every good is His, and thank
> Him for everything . . . (RegNB 17:17f.).

The first gift we receive is the gift of ourselves, our coming into existence as living persons capable of knowledge and love. Francis sees that such a gift comes from the abyss of the Father's love, and he gives thanks to God for Himself ("for yourself": *propter temetipsum*), since he knows that the abyss of divine love is not centered on God Himself but that He created everything because of His "holy will" and His "holy love" (vv. 1-3).

The words "love" and "charity" in Francis's writings nearly always mean the love of the Father and Christ for us, the love that was the motive for creation. Although we are at the pinnacle of God's creation, we are still only part of the "things spiritual and corporal" which the Father created with "His only Son and with the Holy Spirit." The "visible and invisible" world includes the angels who form the nine choirs of tradition (RegNB 23:6), among whom "Blessed Michael, Gabriel, and Raphael" receive special mention. The evil spirits, whom Francis variously calls "devils" (fourteen times), "demons" (three times), "Satan" (twice), "the enemy" (once), are also present where we are working out our salvation.

Francis also speaks about material, "corporal" creation, but he does not do so as much as we would expect from "the patron saint of ecology." In fact, material creation plays only a small part in his writings. Of course, his *Canticle of Brother Sun* gives a striking account of the fraternal presence of the three sets of elements—the sun, moon, and stars; air and water; fire and earth, with fruits, flowers, and herbs. But his references elsewhere in his works to the heavens, earth, sea, abysses, rivers, and birds are taken from the Bible, especially the Psalms. In his *Rule*, he speaks about horses and domestic animals (RegNB 15; cf. RegB 3:12), and in one text (SalVirt), he alludes to "all beasts and wild animals" but says no more about them. Only his *Canticle of Brother Sun* has an original, profound approach to inanimate nature but makes no mention of animals or birds.

In "the image" and "likeness" of God

In two key passages in his writings, Francis declares that we are made in the "image" and "likeness" of God. In his hymn of

thanksgiving for creation (RegNB 23:1), he places us at the summit
of the Father's work:

> You have created all things spiritual and corporal and,
> having made us in your own image and likeness, you placed
> us in paradise.

Again, he admonishes us solemnly:

> Be conscious, O man, of the wondrous state in which the
> Lord God has placed you, for He created you to the image of
> His beloved Son according to the body, and to His likeness
> according to the spirit.

Obviously, Francis was greatly influenced by the idea of our
being made in God's image (Gen 1:26), and he introduced an original
note in this context. We surpass all other created things because we
alone are, as it were, replicas of God, we alone bear His imprint.
When we received from Him "our whole body, our whole soul and
our whole life" (RegNB 23:8), matter and spirit, we became like
Him because we are persons, we are conscious and, most of all, we
are able to love. Between us and God there is a bond of attraction
and resemblance: we call to each other and "need" each other.

In Admonition 5, Francis cries out in surprise and amazement at
the "wondrous state in which the Lord God has placed [us]," and
then he introduces a distinction between "image" and "likeness."
This is a classic distinction, found in the Fathers of the Church (for
example, in Origen and others). According to Francis, by reason of
our bodies, we are not images of the incorporeal and invisible God
but rather of His beloved Son, Jesus, the heavenly prototype of
Adam. When speaking about God's forming the human body,
Francis is not thinking so much about Adam in Genesis as about
every living person. And he implies that God then had before His
eyes the human flesh of His only-begotten Son. Hence the
incomparable dignity of the human body, the first of God's gifts
which Francis mentions (RegNB 23:8). But it is in our "souls," our
"minds," that we are made in the "likeness" of God, although
Francis's Latin text does not make it clear whether this likeness is
to the Son Himself or to God in general. But it is good christology to
regard our bodies as being in the *image* of Christ and our souls in

His *likeness*, or to see the body as the image of the Incarnate Son and the spirit as the image of God. Both interpretations are possible. Francis's originality rests in his thought that we carry the image of the Son in our bodies.

Of the two key passages we are studying (RegNB 23:1; Adm 5:1), the first says explicitly, and the second implies, that the work of creation began with God's "plac[ing] us in paradise" (RegNB 23:1), which is echoed by a reference to "the wondrous state in which the Lord God . . . placed [us]" (Adm 5:1). By using the word "us," Francis boldly depicts us as being present at the creation and in the paradise of the Garden of Eden. In one of his Admonitions (Adm 2), he explains what he means by paradise, from which, "through our own fault, we have fallen" (RegNB 23:2). But so long as we acknowledge that everything we are and everything good we do comes from God, "[we] may eat of the fruit of the trees in the garden" because, when we live "in obedience," we have the broad spaces of true freedom in which to move.

We humans possess our own particular grandeur because we have the incomparable dignity of being formed as images of God and allowed to share in His freedom and happiness. But Francis pauses in the middle of his stately hymn of thanksgiving to remind us that, sadly, "through our own fault we have fallen." We are great, but we are also wretched, so that we could say we possess "greatness in misery." In the following pages, we shall study these two facets of our human existence, our excellence and our downfall, as Francis saw them.

Human Values and Structures

Until recently at least, the English word "man," like the Latin word *homo*, meant a human being of either sex. Francis uses the Latin *homo* seventy-three times in his writings; of these, twenty-two are in the *Earlier Rule* and fourteen in the *Admonitions*. But he also employs feminine terms, the most frequent being the word "mother," twenty-six times, of which six refer to Mary, three to the Christian soul, and two to the Church; "virgin," fifteen times, of which twelve refer to Mary; "woman," seven times; "sister," five times; and "spouse," that is, "wife," once.

He has an astonishingly rich vocabulary to describe the complex human person, at once both spirit and matter. He applies the term "body" primarily to the sacramental Body of Christ (thirty times). He speaks twenty-seven times about the human body in a neutral sense and only sixteen times in the pejorative sense of the body's evil, selfish tendencies. It is almost the same with the word "flesh," which means the material body nine times (six of which refer to the Body of Christ), and only eight times does it have St. Paul's meaning of "this body of death" (Rom 7:24). Francis also mentions various parts of the body, mostly the hands, which he refers to twenty-one times, of which six are to the hands of the priest; also the foot (twelve times), the face (ten times), the eye (seven times), the mouth (six times), the ear (five times), and the head (four times).

The vocabulary he uses when speaking about our spiritual life is more interesting, especially since it differs from our modern usage. Naturally, the word he most frequently employs is "soul," sixty-four times, of which seven appear in the phrase "soul and body." Next in frequency is "heart," used forty-eight times, almost half of which are in quotations from the Bible (nine from the Old Testament and fourteen from the New). "Heart" is also combined with *mens*, "mind, intellect" (five times) and "body" (twice). But the term *mens* (thirteen times) is usually translated as "spirit" since the Latin word *spiritus* is the equivalent of the Greek *noûs*. It means the faculty by which we apprehend and know things, that is, understanding or intelligence. In Francis's writings, the word *spiritus* usually refers to the Holy Spirit and is rarely applied (only five times) to the spiritual element in us, our soul; or it can mean "memory" (five times) or "consciousness, awareness" (twice). Finally, the word "will" occurs twenty-seven times and "desire," good or evil, six times.

We are active beings, and Francis expresses this by words which indicate movement and doing or making things. Here again, his vocabulary is rich and varied, which gives us an indication of his temperament. Of the many verbs he uses, the most common are those which relate to the use of the will, such as "to do" (167 times), "can" or "may" (eighty-nine times), "to will" or "wish" (eighty-three times), "must" or "ought to" (sixty times), "to have to" (forty-one times). Other words express possessing (122 times), giving (sixty-six times) and receiving (sixty times). He uses the verb "to love" fifty times (*amare*, six times; *diligere*, forty-four times), and "to desire" (twelve times). He denotes joy or sadness by "to exult" (thirteen times, all in quotations), "to rejoice" (ten times), "to be joyful" (*laetari*, ten times), "to weep" or "cry" (twice). We can also mention "to say" (146 times) and "to come" (forty-seven times). All this counting may seem tedious, but it does give us some idea of the psychological depth and scope of Francis's thought and language.

Beside speaking about such mundane activities, Francis also specifies the nature of the "paradise" in which God placed us at the beginning. He describes the good things God did and does for us (cf. RegNB 23:8) and will do in the future (2EpFid 61). First, God gave us "our whole body," created in the image of His Son. This should increase our respect for our bodies and lead us to question the popular suspicion that Francis carried asceticism to a morbid extreme and held the body in utter contempt. In fact, he rejoices that God has given us "our whole body, our whole soul," has made us in His own image and draws us to Him (RegNB 23:8). These gifts, the body and soul, are, in a sense, the whole human being who is called to be united with God. Not only that, but God Himself took on these elements of humanity out of love for us humans. Among the many "good things" that God has given us are the beauty of the human body and our intellectual gifts, such as our keenness of mind. He has also given us our spiritual gifts, such as "understand[ing] all mysteries and all knowledge," the knowledge of "tongues" (cf. 1Cor 13:2;14:5), and the gift of miracles (Adm 5:5-7; cf. VPLaet 6). The *Second Letter to the Faithful* (v.83) sums up all these endowments in three words, "talent . . . , power . . . , knowledge" (*talenta, potestas, scientia*). Of course, we pervert these gifts when we regard them as being solely due to our own efforts or when we think we are better than others because of them. Not including the higher gifts of God, such as union with the Trinity, these are the "good things" which God bestows upon us from the beginning.

The Power of Love

One of Francis's most surprising texts occurs at the beginning of the pressing invitation he issues to the various categories of people into which he divides all humanity (RegNB 23:7-11). First, he indicates in a general but comprehensive way the main reason for his appeal: "that all of us may persevere in the true faith and in penance" (v.7). Then, in three successive sections, he explains what he means: everything hinges on *love* of God (v.8) *desire* for God (v.9), and maintaining permanent *contact* with Him (vv.10f.). His invitation is of special interest because, in it, he enumerates twelve ways to love God:

> Let us all love the Lord God with all our heart, all our soul, with all our mind and all our strength, and with fortitude and total understanding, with all our powers, with every effort, every affection, every emotion, every desire, and every wish.

To the seven "powers" listed in the Latin Bible—heart, soul, fortitude or might, mind, strength, understanding, power (Deut 6:5; Mk 12:30,33; Lk 10:27)—Francis added his own—"effort," "affection," "emotion," "desire," and "wish"—because he believed that we can express our love in many different ways since we have extraordinarily diverse inner resources. The commandment in Deuteronomy (6:5) mentions three ways to love God—with heart, soul, and might, which is a summary of our essential humanity, of the things that make us individuals ("heart"), that make us living beings ("soul"), and that allow us to make decisions ("might"). The Synoptic Gospels translate the Hebrew word for "might" by two terms, "strength" (*virtus*) and "powers" (*vires*); and they add "mind" and "understanding" (*dianoia, synesis*). But the original seven terms were apparently not enough for Francis since he adds five others, three of which are connected with the emotions ("affection," "emotion," "desire") and two with the will ("effort," "wish"). The first six terms on his list involve the whole person, while the last six refer to the intensity of will and emotion with which we can love God. Elsewhere (ExpPat 5), Francis also mentions the three powers, "heart, soul, mind." In his eyes, we are capable of great things because God has given us possibilities that are only waiting to be activated.

"To do more and greater things"

In his *Earlier Rule* (17:6), Francis warns his friars about the temptation to think that, because of their good works, they have achieved their purpose in life and are saved: they are "not to take pride in themselves or to delight in themselves, or be puffed up interiorly about their good works and deeds—in fact, about any good thing that God says or does or sometimes works in them." Six of the *Admonitions* repeat this warning almost word for word (Adm 2:3; 8:3; 12:2; 17:1; 21:2; 28:1).

Obviously, Francis saw that, although the friars were heroically living up to the radical demands of their vocation, they still ran the risk of believing that their way of life made them holy and put God in their debt. But, on the other hand, when we consider the positive aspects of the text, we can see that God was working in the friars and doing good in them and through them. Francis recognized that God accomplishes "more and greater things" in all those who put themselves in His hands (2EpFid 36). When we allow God to act in us, we are capable of doing, either in word or action or in the form of spiritual knowledge and insight, "the good things the Lord reveals to [us]" (Adm 21:2; 28:1).

However, Francis does not regard these "good words and good works" as being already done. He describes our sinfulness and poverty in the present tense, that is, as facts. But when he is speaking about the good that has still to be done, he is looking to the future and encourages and urges us to act. Evil is in the present; the good is proposed for the future and is not yet done. Francis's invitations and exhortations to do good are so numerous and insistent only because he believes that we are capable of answering his call. We shall try to summarize the "more and greater things" he proposes to us.

Many passages in the *Earlier Rule* (22:23) and elsewhere call upon us to

> put aside every care and anxiety, to strive as best [we] can
> to serve, love, honor and adore the Lord God with a clean
> heart and a pure mind" (RegNB 22:26). "Let us desire

nothing else, let us wish for nothing else, let nothing else please us and cause us delight except . . . God. . . . Let nothing hinder us, nothing separate us or nothing come between us (RegNB 23:9f.).

This "nothing" is reminiscent of St. John of the Cross's *nada* and shows us how high we must aim. We must allow *nothing* to divert us from union with God. When Francis speaks about our quest, he does so in absolute terms—"nothing" and "above all things" ("Let us desire nothing else. . . . Let us desire above all things" RegNB 17:16; 23:11; RegB 10:8). This is the path to God which he points out to us, a way that is arduous and demanding but still possible.

Similarly, we must, and therefore we can, love our neighbor as Christ did (Jn 15:12; RegNB 11:5), with a love that is both humble and practical like that of a mother (RegNB 9:11; RegB 6:8). This love should lead us, "through the charity of the Spirit," to "serve and obey one another" (RegNB 5:14; RegB 6:8) and to forgive, help, and not be angry with those who sin (RegNB 5:7f.; RegB 7:3; 2EpFid 44; Adm 11:3;14:3; EpMin 1-12). Our love must extend, not only to those who cannot repay us (for example, a sick brother) but also to our enemies, which is the height of love (RegNB 22:1; RegB 10:10; 2EpFid 38; Adm 9; ExpPat 8) and which Francis insists on.

We are called to establish a relationship of love, praise. and service with God and our neighbor and are invited to exercise discernment and spiritual freedom. While Francis's two *Rules* are, as the name implies, documents which lay down rules to be followed, they still leave many decisions to the individual's own judgment (eighteen in the *Earlier Rule* and thirteen in the *Later Rule*). While Francis does not mention "discernment" as such, he does use words and phrases like "spiritually" (eight times), "with the blessing of God" (seven times), "as shall please them" (seven times), "as shall appear to them most expedient" (five times), as well as more general phrases like "they may" and "if they wish," indicating areas in which spiritual freedom may be exercised.

"To reach the Most High"

Our greatness consists both in what we are and what we do. We are made in the image of God, we have been given many gifts, many abilities, many possibilities, and we are called to do great things. But what makes us even greater still is the exalted spiritual experience to which we are invited in this life, even before we complete that experience in the kingdom of God (ExpPat 4). Two texts upon which we have already commented, the *Second Letter to the Faithful* (vv.48-56) and the *Letter to the Entire Order* (vv.50-52), show to what heights God will lead those who love Him.

The rather formal prayer in the *Letter to the Entire Order* (vv.50-52) follows the stages of a journey in which our own actions—knowing, willing, doing, and following in Christ's footsteps—are subordinated to those of the Spirit—purifying, enlightening, and inflaming—so that, solely through the grace of the Father, we finally reach the glory of union with the Trinity.

The *Second Letter to the Faithful* (vv.48-56) focuses more on the role of the Spirit and implies that this union, this spiritual, even mystical, experience is the result of the bonds which the Spirit forges between the Father and the Son and those "men and women" who "persevere to the end," making each one of them a child, spouse, brother, and mother of Christ.

We must understand the "excellence" in which we have been created and established by God and always keep it in mind, since Francis often lays particular stress on the somber side of our fallen nature. He frequently emphasizes the unavoidable truth that we are "wretches and sinners" (RegNB 23:5), so that his estimation of humanity seems to be completely at variance with the incomparable dignity which is ours when we have been enlightened by the Spirit.

Individuals

Francis's view of humanity is not a static but rather a dynamic one, embracing as it does salvation history and the personal spiritual journey of each individual. Our origins are glorious because we are made in the image and likeness of God, and we accomplish and crown His work. Even now we have a share in the paradise in which He "placed" us. But "through our own fault, we have fallen" (RegNB 23:2; 2EpFid 46), and Admonition 2 tells us that our fault consisted in following our own wills and priding ourselves on the good we do.

The root of all our sins is believing that we can be self-sufficient and independent of God. We "appropriate" to ourselves our "own wills" and "exalt [ourselves] over the good things which the Lord says or does in [us]" (Adm 2:3). Instead of the freedom we are looking for, we become "captives," slaves (RegNB 23:3). When Francis wishes to describe our present condition, he uses very strong words which we must admit are true, no matter how harsh and merciless they may seem:

> We should be firmly convinced that nothing belongs to us except our vices and sins, . . . for through our own fault we are rotten, miserable and opposed to good, but prompt and willing to embrace evil. . . . Let us hold ourselves in contempt and scorn, since through our own fault all of us are miserable and contemptible, vermin and worms, . . . wretched, rotten, foul-smelling, ungrateful and evil" (RegNB 17:7; 22:6; 23:8; 2EpFid 46; EpOrd 50; cf. Rev 3:17; Lk 6:35; see parallel passages in RegNB 23:5; 1EpFid 2,3,6).

The diabolical combination "vices and sins" appears twelve times in Francis's writings, especially in the *Letters to the Faithful* (eight times) and in the *Earlier Rule* (twice). As in St. Paul (Gal 5:24: *vitia et concupiscentiae*), the word "vices" means evil tendencies, selfish urges or passions, while "sins" are the voluntary actions which stem from those tendencies. If we list the various words which Francis uses to describe us, we get an ugly-sounding, nauseating catalogue. We are "miserable and contemptible"(quoting Rev 3:17), "ungrateful and evil" (quoting Lk 6:35), "opposed to good," "prompt and willing to embrace evil," "sinners," "rotten," "foul-smelling," "vermin and worms." This reminds us of some texts from St. Paul (for example, Rom 1:28-32; 3:9-20; 1Cor 6:7-11) and especially of the Augustinian tradition on corrupt human nature. Thus the Council of Orange (chap. 22) repeats an Augustinian conclusion that "we have nothing of our own but lies and sins." In his *Confessions*, St. Augustine wrote: "I see that I am ugly, deformed, filthy, covered with blemishes and ulcers. I look at myself and am overcome with disgust." Francis's outlook places him in this tradition, with a strange insistence on rottenness ("rotten," "foul-smelling": three times).

The Source of Evil: the Human Heart

Such a pessimistic view of human nature was not unusual in the
Middle Ages, and Francis was undoubtedly influenced by it.
Moreover, it would seem that his outlook was also the result of
what he had seen in himself and others. Such a combination of
factors would be enough to account for his somber, not to say
thoroughly pessimistic, outlook. Nevertheless, apart from con-
temporaneous influences and his personal experience, he seems to
have been deeply impressed by our Lord's own words about the
evils that come "out of the heart of man" (Mk 7:21), which he
quotes four times (RegNB 22:7; 1EpFid 2:12; 2EpFid 37,69). We are
so greatly inclined and drawn to evil because,

> as our Lord says in the Gospel: "From the heart of man come
> forth and flow evil thoughts, adulteries, fornications,
> murders, thefts, avarice, wantonness, deceit, lewdness, evil
> looks, false testimonies, blasphemy, foolishness." All
> these evil things flow from within, from the heart of a
> person, and those are the things that make a person unclean
> (RegNB 22:7f.).

These thirteen polluted streams—"false testimonies" is an
addition from St. Matthew's Gospel—flow from the same tainted
spring, the human heart. Therefore, Francis's "pessimistic" view of
human nature—if it was pessimism and not clear-sightedness and
realism—did not come primarily from his own experience or other
similar influences. Instead, it was based on an assessment of human
behavior which he found in the Gospels but which is often
overlooked: "For [Christ] Himself knew what was in man" (Jn 2:25),
that he is "ungrateful" and "selfish" (Lk 6:25).

We have already seen the prominent role the human heart
played in Francis's thought, for he regarded it as the unifying
center of the person, the true self, so that, when it is perverted and
turned away from God, it becomes a poisoned well-spring that
corrupts everything. The heart is also both the battlefield and the
trophy to be won in the struggle between God and the enemy, the
devil. Francis insists that we are primarily responsible for the
fall: "Through our own fault we have fallen" (RegNB 23:2). "Even
the demons did not crucify [their Creator], but you, together with

them, have crucified Him and crucify Him even now" (Adm 5:3; cf. *Catechism of the Catholic Church*, n.598, quoting the same text). When we commit sin or suffer some spiritual injury, we are tempted to blame either "the enemy," that is, the devil, or our neighbor. But we must try not to deceive ourselves about who our real enemy is: "Each one has the real enemy in his own power, that is, the body (i.e. his sinful self), through which he sins" (Adm 10).

Yet it is still true that "the devil wishes to take from us the love of Jesus Christ and eternal life" and, in a last desperate effort, "to lose himself with everyone in hell" (RegNB 22:5). The writings provide a keen analysis of the tactics of the devil, who suggests (Adm 2:4), deceives (2EpFid 69), corrupts (RegNB 5:7), and blinds (RegNB 8:4). That is to say, he acts with "malice" and "subtlety":

> He [knows] more about the things of earth than all men together. . . . And wishes that a man not raise his mind and heart to God. And as he roams about, he wishes to ensnare the heart of a person under the guise of some reward or help and to snuff out our memory of the word and precepts of the Lord and wishes to blind the heart of a person through worldly affairs and concerns and to live there" (Adm 5:6; RegNB 22:19f.).

He wants to make us his "children" (1Jn 3:10); 2EpFid 66; RegNB 21:8). Only "Holy Wisdom destroys Satan and all his subtlety, . . . and holy Charity destroys his temptations" (SalVirt 9,13).

"Delighting in sins and vices"

We are capable of doing good, and, in his writings, Francis always represents this good as an aspiration, something to be striven for, a future hope. On the other hand, when he is describing our human condition in the present tense, he does not praise us or encourage us in self-congratulation but rather throws a harsh light on our sinful, degraded condition.

He often uses phrases like "to practice vice and sin" (2EpFid 64) or "to delight in sins and vices" (Adm 5:3) to mean that in doing evil things and taking pleasure in them, we are guilty of a whole series of negative actions and attitudes. A few examples will suffice to illustrate this point. Most frequently mentioned in the

Earlier Rule are failures in regard to our neighbor. Chapter 16, on fraternal charity, gives a long list—slandering, engaging in disputes, quarreling, anger, accusing others, murmuring, detraction, gossiping, judging and condemning others, taking note of their faults. "Anger and trouble of spirit" are constant threats to peace of mind and peace with others (Adm 11:3; 14:3; 27:2; RegNB 5:7f.; RegB 7:3; 2EpFid 44; VPLaet 15).

Admonition 27 not only provides a catalogue of virtues but also lists the sins opposed to them: fear and ignorance, anger and disturbance; covetousness and avarice; anxiety and dissipation; excess and hardness of heart. Nor did Francis fail to mention sexual attraction and what it can lead to: impure glances and desires, fornication (RegNB 12:13). On the negative side of the two ways of life which he describes (2EpFid 63-69), he gives a list of sins:

> All those . . . who are not living in penance and do not receive the Body and Blood of our Lord Jesus Christ, who practice vice and sin and walk the paths of wicked concupiscence and evil desires, who do not observe what they have promised and bodily serve the world by the desires of the flesh, the cares and anxieties of this world and the preoccupations of this life—such people are deceived by the devil, whose children they are and whose works they perform. They are blind.

And these people are to be held to account because "they see and acknowledge, they know and do evil and knowingly they lose their souls" (v.68). The type of conduct which Francis describes here shows that he had no illusions about human nature and that his psychological insight was comparable to that demonstrated by the Fathers of the Desert in their rules and practices.

Appropriating the Good that God Does

The real evil consists, not in those sins which we acknowledge as such, but in using good things for evil purposes. It is bad enough when we do not acknowledge the good things which the Lord does in and through us. But Francis's worst fear was that, instead of acknowledging the source of that good by an act of praise, an "act of thanksgiving," we would attribute it to ourselves by "appropriating" it (used three times). Anyone who does this "eats of the tree of knowledge of good [by] appropriat[ing] to himself his own will and thus exalts himself over the good things which the Lord says and does in him" (Adm 2:3). If we think that we owe our existence and our faith to ourselves alone, then we are committing Original Sin all over again by imitating Adam and acting as if we were God, as if we were self-sufficient and completely independent of everyone. We must, therefore, regard nothing as our own, neither material possessions (RegNB 7:13; RegB 6:1), nor authority over others (Adm 4:1; RegNB 17:4), nor the office of preaching (RegNB 17:4), and especially not our own "wills" (Adm 2:3), that is, in the general context of this Admonition, our very selves. Nor are we to attribute to ourselves our spiritual knowledge of Scripture because, if we do not "return" it to the Lord, to whom everything good belongs, it becomes the "letter that kills" (2Cor 3:6; Adm 7:1,4).

The first consequence of what Francis considers a theft akin to that of Judas (Jn 12:6; Adm 4:3) is "pride and vainglory" (RegNB 17:9; RegB 10:7), the result of which he expressed by the verb "to exalt oneself," to be self-important, self-sufficient (Adm 2:3;12:2; 17:1). Admonition 5 shows how foolish is this pretense:

> In what . . . can you glory? For if you were so subtle and wise that you had all knowledge and knew how to interpret all tongues and minutely investigate the course of the heavenly bodies . . . ; if you were more handsome and richer than everyone else, and even if you performed wonders such as driving out demons, . . . none of [this] would belong to you nor could you glory in any of these things (vv.4-7).

Francis begs the friars, who are especially exposed to this temptation,

> not to take pride in themselves or to delight in themselves or be puffed up interiorly about their good words and deeds—in fact, about any good thing that God does or says or sometimes works in them and through them (RegNB 17:6).

This pride arises because:

> the spirit of the flesh desires and is most eager to have words, but cares little to carry them out. And it does not seek a religion and holiness in the interior spirit, but it wishes and desires to have a religion and holiness outwardly apparent to people (RegNB 17:11f.).

The friar who is motivated by this spirit

> does not keep in his heart the good things the Lord reveals to him and does not manifest them to others by his actions, but rather seeks to make such good things known by his words . . . . Therefore, it is a great shame for us, servants of God, that, while the saints actually did such things, we wish to receive glory and honor by merely recounting their deeds (Adm 21:2; 28; 6:3).

This attitude has sad consequences for our relationship with our neighbor since it makes us envious. The good things which our neighbor has done make us sad because we did not do them ourselves. Francis puts the friars on their guard against this vice (RegB 10:7) and bluntly describes its real nature: "Whoever envies his brother the good which the Lord says or does in him commits a sin of blasphemy because he envies the Most High who says and does every good" (Adm 8:3). Instead of being saddened by envy or jealousy, we should "rejoice in the good fortune of others as well as our own" (ExpPat 5). And no one should "wish to receive more from his neighbor than what he is willing to give of himself to the Lord God" (ExpPat 5; Adm 17:2).

Francis portrays our human wretchedness so harshly because he wants to contrast it with God's unconditioned love, which he describes in this oft-quoted text:

> Let us all love the Lord God with all our heart, all our soul, with all our mind and all our strength and with fortitude and with total understanding, with all of our powers, with every effort, every affection, every emotion, every desire and every wish. He has given and gives to each one of us our whole body, our whole soul and our whole life. He created us and redeemed us and will save us by His mercy

alone. He did and does every good thing for us (RegNB 23:8).

By such unrelenting insistence on our sinful state, Francis wishes to inspire in us the pure gratitude of complete love. To this end also he suggests a path of conversion which will lead us out of our "wretchedness," and he warns us that, if we do not repent and be converted, we are in danger of being eternally damned.

Eternal Damnation

Because we have free will, we can reject salvation but, as our Lord warns us, by such a rejection we deny Him and put ourselves on the road to eternal damnation:

> Those who do not wish to taste how sweet the Lord is and love the darkness rather than the light, not wishing to fulfill the commands of God, are cursed; of them the prophet says: "They are cursed who stray from your commands" (2EpFid 16f.).

The dramatic scene at the General Judgment (Mt 25:31-46) as the damned are cast into eternal fire was much in Francis's thoughts. In fact, unlike the Gospel (Mt 25:34), he mentions the damnation of the wicked before the glorification of the righteous. The Son

> will come . . . in the glory of His majesty to send the wicked ones who have not done penance and who have not known you into the eternal fire. . . . "Come, you blessed of my Father" (RegNB 23:4).

The close of the *Canticle of Brother Sun* follows the same order: "Woe to those who die in mortal sin. Blessed are those whom death will find in your most holy will" (CantSol 13), while Francis's third description of the Last Day (RegNB 21:8f.), follows the order of the Gospel: "Blessed. . . . Cursed. . . ."

The motives for refusing to do God's will and the unhappy consequences are ours alone, not God's. Dying "in mortal sin" is the result of not having done penance and not knowing God (RegNB 23:4; 21:8). We have been deceived by the devil and have become his "children" by doing his works (Jn 8:41; RegNB 21:8); we are blind and have no spiritual understanding. That is why we are lost, not by chance, but by our own deliberate personal choice: "[We] see and acknowledge, [we] know and do evil and knowingly lose [our] souls" (2EpFid 66-68). Francis portrays this final loss by using the traditional images found in Scripture: "eternal fire" (RegNB 21:8; 23:4; 11:4), "hell" (1EpFid 2:18; 2EpFid 85; RegNB 22:5; EpRect 5), "the second death" (Rev 20:6; CantSol 13), "punishment" (EpRect 5), "tormented" (1EpFid 2:18; 2EpFid 85), and the exclamation "Woe!" (*Vae!*—RegNB 21:8).

The damnation of the unrepentant sinner is recounted dramatically in the *Second Letter to the Faithful*:

> Whenever or however a person dies in mortal sin without making amends when he could have done so and did not, the devil snatches up his soul out of his body with so much anguish and tribulation that no one can know it unless he has experienced it. . . . Worms eat his body. And so he loses body and soul . . . and will go down to hell, where he will be tormented without end (vv.82,85).

The sections of Francis's writings which deal with eternal damnation can be divided into two categories. Three passages deal with salvation in general and the ultimate choice we must make (RegNB 21:8; 23:4; CantSol 13), while three others (1EpFid 2:15,18; 2EpFid 82,85; EpRect 3,5) are part of an appeal to the sinner, telling him what is at stake and placing before him the choice he must make. Francis was well aware of the risk to which the human will is exposed and, as did Christ in the Gospel, he solemnly confronts us with our responsibility.

The image-filled, rhetorical language which Francis uses, especially in the *Letters to the Faithful*, is that of the Gospels and of his own time, language which we might hesitate to use nowadays even though it does focus our attention on the gravity of the consequences of our final choice. But, on the other hand, the glorious results of a right choice on our part—conversion, salvation, and eternal happiness—also occupy an important place in Francis's message. In the following chapter, we shall deal with the path of conversion that leads to happiness in this life and the next.

The Community of the Church

So far, we have been considering Francis's thoughts on our wretchedness and our greatness as individuals. Now we shall try to see what he has to say about the individual in the context of a large group or community, for, although he does not deal specifically with this point, by no means does he neglect it. It is true that he is mainly concerned with the individual as a member of the community of the Church on earth and in heaven. Yet this does not prevent him from referring to social and even political situations, as we have seen above when we were discussing the contents and classification of his writings.

Having examined Francis's views on the individual, we must now consider the way he sees the Church of which he wishes us to be faithful children. This Church, with her structures and her mystery, exists here on earth, as well as on high, in the Communion of Saints, over which our glorious Lady, the Virgin Mary, presides.

The Church on Earth

Francis mentions the Church with relative frequency in his writings (twenty-two times). Mostly he calls it "holy" (ten times), at other times "Roman" (five times), "mother" (twice), catholic and apostolic. By the term "Catholic" (thirteen times), he means being faithful to the Church's teachings and discipline, while by "Christian" he indicates belonging to, being a member of, the Church. When he is writing about the "personnel" of the Church, his vocabulary is naturally wider, since he has to refer to the many different categories of people in the Church. He speaks about priests (thirty-two times), clerics (twenty-eight times), religious (fourteen times), lay people (twelve times), the Pope (nine times), bishops (eight times), prelates (seven times), the Apostolic See (twice), cardinals (once), theologians (once), and the Roman Curia (once). He was well acquainted with the complexities of the institutional Church of his day, which he depicts as being decidedly "clerical." It is interesting to note that those texts which refer in any way to the mystery of the Church occur in his rules for living the truly Christian life (Adm 26; 2EpFid 33-35; RegNB

Prol.; 19:20; 23:7; RegB 1:12; Test 4-13). This implies that, for him, the Christian life can have no meaning except within the Christian community and guided by its ministers.

The Mystery of the Church

Although the terminology which Francis uses seems quite "institutional," he still portrays the Church as based on the mystery of the Trinity and composed of the people of God.

In the *Salutation of the Blessed Virgin Mary*, he addresses Mary, as the "virgin made church," a glorious title for our Lady since it shows her as the anticipation, the figure or icon of the Church. Already she is what the Church will be in its fullness at the end of time. Francis's hymn of praise goes on to salute Mary as "chosen by the Father . . . , consecrated [by Him], with His most holy beloved Son and . . . the Holy Spirit the Paraclete." Because of this, "there was and is all the fullness of grace and every good" in her, and Francis can acclaim her as the "Palace . . . , Tabernacle . . . , [and] Robe" of God, as well as His "Mother" and "Servant." But since our Lady has all the characteristics of the Church, what Francis says about her applies also to the Church. The most profound attribute of the Church, then, is the fact that she has been chosen and consecrated by the Trinity, thus making her the dwelling place of God, bearing the Lord and His Gospel, at once a humble, obedient servant and the glorious mother of life. The fundamental mystery of the Church is based on the Trinity and Mary.

But the Church is also a physical reality made up of *the people of God*. This community aspect, which modern ecclesiology emphasizes, is well described in the *Earlier Rule* (23:7), where Francis portrays a procession led by the seven ranks of the clergy, who are followed by fifteen different categories of people, each composed of paired groups:

> . . . All those who wish to serve the Lord God within the holy, catholic and apostolic church, and all the following orders: priests, deacons, subdeacons, acolytes, exorcists, lectors, porters and all clerics, all religious men and all religious women, all lay brothers and youths (in the monasteries), the poor and the needy, kings and princes,

workers and farmers, servants and masters, all virgins and
continent and married women, all lay people, men and
women, all children, adolescents, the young and the old,
the healthy and the sick, all the small and the great, all
peoples, races, tribes and tongues, all nations and all
peoples everywhere on earth who are and who will be.

As Francis sees it, the Church is an immense crowd in which the
poor, the unimportant people, and the children hold first place but
in which the hierarchy, priests, and clerics, and the various social
structures are also included. The group takes into account the age,
sex, and state of health of its members and contains within it
people of the present time and of the times to come. All these form
the Church in which they wish to serve the Lord God "in the true
faith and in penance."

The *hierarchical structure* of this Church stands out quite
clearly, so clearly, in fact, that, at first glance, it seems to be too
"clericalized." "The Lord Pope" (Innocent III and Honorius III)
approved the *Rule*, and Francis promised "obedience and
reverence" to him (RegNB Prol; RegB 1). While the bishops are
prominent in the Church (RegB 2:4;9:11), the priests and clerics are
mentioned most often and, because of their office as ministers of the
word and the sacraments (2EpFid 34), they must be shown
reverence, love, and honor. As the people of God travel on their
spiritual journey, they form the various ranks which Francis knows
and respects. He and his Fraternity are part of this Church, and he
has a surprisingly balanced understanding of its complexity. He
declares that "No one showed me what I should do, but the Most
High Himself revealed to me that I should live according to the
form of the Holy Gospel" (Test 14). Then he presented himself
before the Pope to ask him to approve and confirm his *Rule* for
living the life of the Gospel (RegNB Prol 2). On this point, both
Rules show his determination to plant the Franciscan Fraternity
deep in the basic structure of "the Holy Roman Church . . . so that,
steadfast in the Catholic faith, we may observe the poverty and
the humility and the holy Gospel of our Lord Jesus Christ" (RegB
12:4).

It remains for us to examine Francis's writings for his views on
the functions of the Church and on what it brings to the faithful.

Its first service is to be the place of faith and Gospel conversion, as Francis tells us in his *Earlier Rule*: ". . . so that all of us may persevere in the true faith and in penance, for otherwise no one will be saved" (RegNB 23:7). "The true faith" consists in our marveling appreciation of all that God has done for us, as the first verses of chapter 23 of the same *Rule* proclaim (vv.1-4). Faith is then followed by a life transformed and renewed by "penance" or conversion. The Church's first function, therefore, is to meet this double need—faith and conversion.

The Church is also the place in which the Son of God is present. Only through the ministry of its priests (2EpFid 35) is the Body and Blood of the Son of the Most High God made present, "through which we have been made and have been redeemed from death to life" (EpCler 3). Moreover, the Church is *the criterion of faith*, so that the faithful must be Catholics, living and speaking as such and never straying from Catholic life and faith (RegNB 19:1f.; 2EpFid 32). Those who wish to be part of the Fraternity must be Catholics (RegB 2:2), otherwise they will be expelled (RegNB 19:2; Test 31). The Gospel life meant more to Francis than anything else; yet all he demanded from priests of dubious moral conduct was that they should be orthodox, which, in the context, meant being orthodox in *faith* at least, if not in *practice* (2EpFid 33; Test 6; Adm 26:1f). Finally, the Church is *the norm of conduct*, and we must comply with its requirements, even the solely disciplinary ones. We must not do anything "contrary to the form and the prescriptions of the Holy Church" (RegNB 2:12; 17:1). On the contrary, we must observe "the constitutions of holy Mother Church" (EpCler 30) concerning the celebration of Mass (EpOrd 30) with due respect (1EpCust 4); concerning liturgical prayer (Test 31); and the canonical regulations regarding the religious life (RegNB 2:10; RegB 2:2,4,12). Such strictness may seem surprising in a man like Francis, who is so often regarded as being "charismatic" and "a free spirit." But his attitude was based on his deep faith in the Church, a faith that included acceptance of its structures, its laws, and even its frailties. For him, "holy Mother Church," as well as being a tangible reality, was also the place where God, His Son, His Gospel, and His sacraments are to be found, since, like Mary, the Church is the "Home" and the "Robe" of God.

With great acumen, Francis had grasped the theological essence of the Church, the fact that it is rooted in the Trinity and is the people of God, even including its institutional structures! He saw both sides of the picture. While he sometimes had to contend with the dead weight of a worldly Church in the form of the incompetence, corruption, and opposition of the clergy, he still believed with all his heart in a Church that has within it the Son of God and His Gospel, the guarantee of "the true faith and penance."

The Church in Heaven

Francis's vision extended as far as the end of time and beyond. He looked towards the Second Coming of Christ in glory and majesty (RegNB 23:4), for which we must always be alert and watchful (RegNB 9:14; 22:27). But he also was aware of "the eschatology of the present," which, free of the limitations of time and space, is already here and accessible to faith. Besides the Crucified and Risen Lord, "He who is now not about to die but who is eternally victorious and glorified, upon whom the angels desire to gaze" (EpOrd 22), this "present" includes what we can refer to as the Church in heaven. Francis calls upon this "Church" to join with the Son and the Paraclete in their hymn of thanksgiving to the Father for His wonderful works (RegNB 23:6):

> . . . the glorious Mother, most blessed Mary ever-virgin, Blessed Michael, Gabriel and Raphael and all the blessed choirs of seraphim, cherubim, thrones, dominations, principalities, powers, virtues, angels, archangels, blessed John the Baptist, John the Evangelist, Peter, Paul, and the blessed patriarchs, prophets, the Innocents, apostles, evangelists, disciples, martyrs, confessors, virgins, the blessed Elijah and Henoch, and all the saints who were, who will be, and who are.

Although we have already quoted this passage, it deserves repetition and further comment. Francis's vision begins at the summit, where "the glorious Mother, most blessed Mary ever-virgin" sits enthroned. Mary occupies a pre-eminent place in Francis's writings, as his vocabulary shows. When describing our

Lady, he uses no less than twenty different terms. She is the "virgin" (ten times) and "mother" (five times), the "servant" (twice), as well as the "lady" and "queen." She is the daughter of the Father, chosen by Him; she is "the spouse of the Holy Spirit" and "the virgin made church." Adjectives such as "holy" (eight times), "blessed" (seven times), "glorious" (three times) abound when Francis speaks about her.

Whenever Francis contemplates the mystery of God and all His work in the world (RegNB 23:1-6; 2EpFid 4-14), Mary is present also. She is, as it were, the dividing line between before and after, the door through which salvation came into the world. The Father sent His word (cf. 2EpFid 4) and "brought about His birth . . . by the glorious, ever-virgin, most blessed, holy Mary" (RegNB 23:3: note the four adjectives; cf. OffPass Ps 15:3). "In the womb of the holy and glorious Virgin Mary, [the Word] received the flesh of our humanity and our frailty" (2EpFid 4f.; RegNB 9:5; UltVol 1). She is "honored as is right . . . since she carried Him in her most holy womb" (EpOrd 21). Francis explicitly dedicated two poems to Mary, the antiphon of praise to be said before and after each psalm in his *Office of the Passion*, and a salute in the courtly manner, the *Salutation of the Blessed Virgin Mary*:

> Holy Virgin Mary, among women there is no one like you born into the world: you are the daughter and the servant of the most high and supreme King and Father of heaven, you are the mother of our most holy Lord Jesus Christ, you are the spouse of the Holy Spirit. Pray for us . . . to your most holy beloved Son, the Lord and Master" (AntOffPass).

The remarkable feature of this text is the relationship it establishes between Mary and the Three Divine Persons. She is unique among women because the bond between her and the Father makes her His daughter and, at the same time, His servant; that is to say, she has been elevated far above the rest of humanity, yet she still remains human. She alone can be called the Mother of God because she is the mother of the Lord Jesus. When the Holy Spirit overshadowed her (Lk 1:35), she became His spouse. Since this mystery of relationship with the Trinity was fully realized in Mary, it extends also to all the faithful. In fact, Francis gave the same titles, "daughter, mother and spouse," practically word for word, to St. Clare and her sisters (FormViv 1f.).

Francis's salute to Mary was a solemn one:

> Hail, O Lady, holy Queen, Mary, holy Mother of God: you are the virgin made church and the one chosen by the most holy Father in heaven whom He consecrated with His most holy beloved Son and with the Holy Spirit the Paraclete, in whom there was and is all the fullness of grace and every good. Hail, His Palace! Hail, His Tabernacle! Hail, His Home! Hail, His Robe! Hail, His Servant! Hail, His Mother!

Here Francis sees Mary as the majestic virgin of a Roman sculpture. Lady, Queen, and Virgin-made-Church, she is no ordinary woman but the holy Mother of God (*Dei Genitrix*, the Latin equivalent of the Greek *Théotokos*), the title which signifies her incomparable dignity. As in Francis's antiphon in his *Office of the Passion*, here Mary's relationships with the Trinity are repeated. The Father chose her, and, in a solemn concelebration with the Son and the Paraclete, He consecrated her like a church. She who is "full of grace" has received and retains within her "all the fullness of grace and every good," that is, the Son of God, "full of grace and truth" (Jn 1:14).

Mary's greatness is based on her relationships with the Triune God and the "fullness" which is always hers. Francis salutes her under six different titles: "Palace," a spacious, sumptuous building; "Tabernacle," a sacred tent housing the Ark of the Covenant; "Home," the humble, ordinary family dwelling. Furthermore, she is the "Robe" that clothes God and is the cloak of His humanity. The title of "Servant" is the only one which Mary gave herself (Lk 1:38-48); and, finally, she is "His Mother." This contemplative hymn presents a tableau in which the *Théotokos* stands before the Church in the humble role of a servant, while the Father, Son, and Holy Spirit consecrate and crown her. That is how Francis contemplates the luminous yet humble depths of the mystery of Mary.

Although Mary is so close to her Son, to the Father, and to the Holy Spirit, she is still part of the "great cloud of witnesses" (Heb 12:1) which forms the Church in heaven. Gathered closest around her are the angels, divided into the nine choirs of tradition and presided over by their three leaders, Michael, Gabriel, and Raphael. Michael, the warrior, seems to have been Francis's special favorite, since he invokes him elsewhere also (AntOffPass 3; ExhLD 17); and he mentions Gabriel as the messenger of the Incarnation (2EpFid 4). The angels are spiritual beings created by God, who is "in Heaven, in the angels and in the saints, enlightening them . . . , inflaming them to love . . . , and filling them with happiness" (ExpPat 2).

After Mary and the angelic ranks of her heavenly court, the first figure to emerge from the crowd is that of John the Baptist, than whom "there has risen no one greater" (Mt 11:11). A Byzantine antiphon, quoted by Francis, tells us that, when baptizing Christ, John "trembled and did not dare to touch the holy head of God" (EpOrd 21). After the Baptist comes John, the beloved disciple and evangelist. Perhaps because Francis's own baptismal name was John, he did not follow the usual order of precedence but placed John before Peter and Paul. Then follow, in the order of the Litany of the Saints, the different categories which are meant to include all forms of sanctity: patriarchs, prophets, the Holy Innocents, apostles, evangelists, disciples, martyrs, confessors, and virgins. Next Francis gives two names, Elijah and Henoch, who are not usually included in such lists. They are called "the saints of the last day," for they are not dead (Gen 5:24; 2Kings 2:11), but will come again at the end of time. Those who are dying invoke their aid in entering eternal life. Francis's tendency to universalism leads him to cast his net even wider, for he calls upon "all the saints who were, or who will be, or who are," while, in another passage, he invokes "all the saints in heaven and on earth" (EpOrd 38). Thus, he looks at the present and the future, at heaven and earth, all at once, as if he were seeing with the eyes of God. He mentions saints who followed Christ along especially difficult paths (Adm 6:3), confesses his sins before them (EpOrd 38), and asks for their intercession (AntOffPass 2; ExpPat 7) and their blessing (Test 40).

Between the two "Churches," on earth and on high, there is constant communication and exchange, even familiarity. Together, they include everything spiritual and corporal (Reg 23:1). The

Church on earth is built around the Presence of Christ, that is, around His word and His sacramental Body; and it is formed of men and women of all times, gathered together, with "the priests, clerics and theologians." This Church is hierarchical and visible, even sinful; yet it is founded upon the fact that it has been chosen by the Father and consecrated by the Son and the Paraclete. Its very existence remains an object of faith here below, but is already manifested on high in the Communion of Saints, thronging around the majestic throne of Mary, "the humblest and the most exalted of creatures" (Dante).

Francis's "ecclesiology," his theology of the Church, contains the basic vision of that Church as being holy, despite its shortcomings, and indispensable, as the only place where the Gospel and salvation are to be found.

Chapter 5

The Christian Journey

We humans are a combination of opposites, a mixture of greatness and wretchedness. Although we are made for the fullness of life and happiness in heaven, we can still descend to "delighting in vices and sins" (Adm 5:3) which lead to our damnation. But out of love for us, God freed us from the slavery of sin by the Blood of His Son; and the Son, living now no more to die, draws us after Him and offers us salvation by giving us Himself. "His yoke is sweet and His burden light . . . " for those who "taste how sweet the Lord is" (2EpFid 12-16). In his *Second Letter to the Faithful*, Francis first describes the work of salvation accomplished by Christ (vv.3-12) and then goes on to propose to every Christian a new way of life, the principal stages of which we have already analyzed briefly above (See, Foundation: The Father sends the Word, p. 39). We shall now re-examine this text and describe in more detail the mode of life by which we can serve the Lord "in the true faith and in penance" (RegNB 23:7). As we have seen, the actions and attitudes demanded by a change of life ("penance," conversion) are always inspired by our awareness of what God is and what He has done and still does for us ("the true faith").

"With our hearts turned to the Lord"

We shall begin with what our Lord calls "the great and first commandment" (Mk 12:28-31; Mt 22:38), on which Francis comments as follows:

> Let us love God, therefore, and adore Him with a pure heart and a pure mind because He who seeks this above all else has said: The true worshippers will adore the Father in spirit and in truth (Jn 4:23). For all those who worship Him are to worship Him in the spirit of truth (cf. Jn 4:24). And let us praise Him and pray to Him day and night (Ps 31:4), saying: Our Father, who are in heaven

> (Mt 6:9), since we should pray always and never
> lose heart (Lk 18:1) (2EpFid 19-21).

Francis composed this passage mainly from biblical quotations and addressed it to all Christians, while, for his friars, he wrote a parallel but more detailed description of the Gospel life in his *Earlier Rule*:

> Therefore, all my brothers, let us be very much on our guard so that we do not lose or turn away our minds and hearts from the Lord under the guise of achieving some reward or doing some work or providing some help. But in the holy love which is God, I beg all my brothers, both the ministers and the others, as they overcome every obstacle and put aside every care and anxiety, to strive as best they can to serve, love, honor and adore the Lord God with a clean heart and a pure mind, for this is what He desires above all things. And let us make a home and dwelling place (cf. Jn 14:23) for Him who is the Lord God Almighty, Father and Son and Holy Spirit, who says: Watch, therefore, praying constantly that you may be considered worthy to escape all the evils that are to come and to stand secure before the Son of Man. And when you stand to pray, say: Our Father who art in heaven. And let us adore Him with a pure heart, because we should pray always and not lose heart; for the Father seeks such worshippers. God is Spirit, and those who worship Him must worship Him in spirit and in truth (RegNB 22:25-31).

Francis sees that our primary and most "visceral" reaching out to God has many facets, the first of which is love (RegNB 23:8; 1EpFid 1:1; 2EpFid 18f.). In his *Prayer Inspired by the Our Father*, he lists the precise demands of this love:

> That we may love you with our whole heart by always thinking of you; with our whole soul by always desiring you; with our whole mind by directing all our intentions to you and by seeking your glory in everything; and with all our strength by spending all our energies and affections of soul and body in the service of your love and of nothing else (ExpPat 5).

However, love is far from being the only component of this surge of the heart towards God. In fact, Francis uses the verb "to adore" some fifteen times in his writings, and both the texts under discussion here insist strongly on adoration as an attitude of awe, extreme reverence, and prostration of soul and body before the majesty of God. Yet adoration is not primarily our own work but that of the Spirit, who alone adores the Father in truth, as the texts from St. John's Gospel make clear. Francis adds other expressions, such as "honor" and "serve," especially with "a clean heart and a pure mind," which we must never "turn away . . . from the Lord" (RegNB 22:19,25). Such attitudes lead us to the mystery of union with God: "Let us make [in our hearts] a home and dwelling place for Him, who is the Lord God Almighty, Father and Son and Holy Spirit" (RegNB 22:27).

This link between God and us goes far beyond what we ordinarily call prayer and takes two forms. The first form is an interior, personal, continuous bond. It is expressed especially by the terms "to adore," "to watch," "not to lose heart," as well as by the texts from St. John. The second form of this link is a communitarian one which is succinctly expressed in the Our Father and which is implied in Francis's invitation: "Let us praise Him and pray to Him day and night" (2EpFid 21).

In the writings which he addresses to the friars, Francis regards liturgical prayer as a basic element of their life (RegNB 3; RegB 3; Test 18,29,31), and, in his *Letter to the Entire Order*, he indicates the way it should be celebrated: "so that the voice may blend with the mind and the mind be in harmony with God" (EpOrd 41-43).

When writing here and elsewhere about our contact with God, that is, our spiritual experiences, Francis uses a specific vocabulary (cf. also Adms 1, 16). The word he uses most frequently in this context is "heart" (thirty-one times out of a total of forty-eight), followed by *mens* ("mind," "spirit"—five times) or its equivalent *animus* (twice), while he also refers to "memory." To describe the movements of the heart that is "turned to the Lord," he borrows some of the words found in St. John—"to see" (twenty-five times), "to love" (eighteen times), "to know" (sixteen times), "to believe" (sixteen times), as well as others expressing desire, such as "to seek" (five times), "to desire" (four times) and "to delight in" (twice). As we have seen, Francis's prayers are almost exclusively prayers in praise of God, containing such words as "to praise" (twenty-three times), "to bless" (sixteen times), "to adore" (fifteen times), "to beseech" (fifteen times), "to exalt" (fifteen times), "to thank" (thirteen times), "to honor" (seven times), "to magnify" (six times), and "to glorify" (twice).

These prayers, some fifteen in all, show us better than any sermon how to approach God. Except for the *Prayer Before the Crucifix*, they are all essentially contemplative. In them, we marvel at, and thank God for, His wonderful plans (RegNB 23:1-6). We try, and fail, to express the inexpressible ardor of our encounter with Him (LaudDei). We review the spiritual journey we must take (EpOrd 50-52), and, above all, we use fervent invitatories to call upon the whole of creation to praise and rejoice in God and the Blessed Virgin (RegNB 17:17-19; 21:2; 23:7-11; LaudHor; ExhLD; 2EpFid 61f.; OffPass, Prayer; CantSol; SalBMV; and AntOffPass).

The texts which describe our relationship with God— especially Adm 1; RegNB 22; 2EpFid 48f.—and which we can call prayers, give us a comprehensive view of what prayer itself is. The source or origin of prayer is the Spirit, who dwells in and rests upon the faithful (Adm 1:12; 2EpFid 48), making them the "home and dwelling" of the Trinity. The Spirit, the true Adorer of the Father, produces in those in whom He resides an inclination to reach out to God, a movement "of holy prayer and devotion" (RegB 5:2). By His "holy manner of working," the Spirit urges those in whom He dwells to pray with a pure heart (RegB 10:8f.) and with all the diversity and richness that such prayer implies. This prayer of the Spirit occurs when:

> wherever we are . . . , [we] continually believe truly and humbly and keep in our heart and love, honor, adore, serve, praise and bless, glorify and exalt, magnify and give thanks to the most high and supreme eternal God, Trinity and Unity, the Father and the Son and the Holy Spirit (RegNB 23:11).

Here, as always, the center of our prayer is the Triune God, to whom our hearts respond fervently with different movements and sentiments (the text lists twelve), culminating in a threefold outburst of praise—"the most high and supreme eternal God: Trinity and Unity: the Father and the Son and the Holy Spirit."

If we are to succeed in praying continually, everywhere, and in every situation, we must have pure hearts. Francis tells us what a pure heart is when he comments on the beatitude in St. Matthew's Gospel (5:8):

> Blessed are the pure of heart, for they shall see God. The truly pure of heart are those who despise the things of earth and seek the things of heaven, and who never cease to adore and behold the Lord God living and true with a pure heart and soul (Adm 16).

So, according to Francis, only those whose hearts have been so enlightened that they spurn earth and seek heaven alone can truly adore and behold God. That is to say, adoration precedes vision. Our hearts are pure when we view earthly things from "on high," that is, when we see their true value, when we "despise" them. This Latin word, *despicere*, is taken from a contemporary liturgical text, the postcommunion of the Second Sunday in Advent. And our hearts are pure when we "seek the things of heaven," that is, when we search for the mystery present in everything, a mystery whose very center is God Himself. These demands are difficult to meet since they require us to rid ourselves of everything that is an obstacle to a truly spiritual life—worldly cares, anxiety, and self-justification. But when we surrender ourselves docilely to the Spirit's "holy manner of working" (RegB 10:7), then our whole lives are transformed, and everything we do (Adm 3:4), provided it is right and good, follows "the will of the Lord" and "please[s] Him" (RegNB 22:9).

"We must . . . be Catholics" (2EpFid 32)

We have already described what Francis understood by the Church. Here we shall confine ourselves to discussing how he saw life in the Church of his times, especially as regards reception of the sacraments and the attitude of the ordinary faithful towards the clergy who administered these sacraments.

In his account of the demands of the Christian life, he first appeals to us to love and adore God, and then, immediately after, he tells us that we must confess our sins and receive communion (2EpFid 22-24). In his writings, he also mentions baptism, but only twice and then very briefly—Christ's baptism (EpOrd 21) and the baptism to which nonbelievers are invited "to be born again of water and the Holy Spirit" and so "enter into the kingdom of God" (cf. Jn 3:5; RegNB 16:7). The fact that he quotes St. John shows that he had a proper understanding of the nature of baptism; but he does not refer to this sacrament elsewhere in his writings.

In contrast, penance, or the confession of sins, plays a large part in Francis's work. In his *Second Letter to the Faithful*, he warns us that "We must also confess all our sins to a priest" (2EpFid 22), "Confess all your sins" (RegNB 21:6), and then he describes dramatically the dying sinner's refusal to repent and make restitution (2EpFid 77-81). Following the custom in the Middle Ages, the friars often went to confession but encountered difficulties when priests were unavailable. No wonder, then, that the texts which Francis addressed to the friars frequently deal with this sacrament. He devotes a chapter to it in each of his *Rules*, and, in his *Letter to a Minister*, he writes at length about it.

In chapter 20 of his *Earlier Rule*, he gently exhorts his friars: "My blessed brothers, both the clerics as well as the lay, should confess their sins to priests of our Order." He then goes on to take various circumstances into consideration. If a friar-priest is not available, the brothers may confess to any Catholic priest, an anti-heretical measure (v.2). And if no priest is to be found, "they may confess to their brother, as the apostle James says" (v.3). Francis, therefore, knew about and approved of "lay confession," but he immediately urged the friars "to have recourse to a priest since the power of binding and loosing is granted only to priests" (v.4).

His *Letter to a Minister*, drafted before the *Later Rule* was composed, contains almost the same directions—confession to a priest, or, failing that, to a brother—but it makes a distinction between venial sins and the grave sins which were reserved to a higher superior for absolution. The *Later Rule* made provision for reserved sins for which a friar had to have recourse to the Minister for absolution and penance; and here Francis does not mention "lay confession." In his *Earlier Rule*, when he is speaking about fraternal correction (RegNB 5:3-8), and especially in his *Letter to a Minister*, we see his tender mercy towards sinners:

> All the brothers who might know that [one of their brothers] has sinned are not to bring shame upon him or speak ill of him, but let them show great mercy towards him and keep most secret the sin of their brother, because i t is not the healthy who are in need of the physician, but those who are sick (Mt 9:12; EpMin 15; RegNB 5:8).

Francis saw that in these circumstances nothing is worse than "being disturbed or angered" since that only spreads the evil. He puts us on our guard against this danger no fewer than six times (Adm 11:3; 14:3; VPLaet 15; RegNB 5:7; RegB 7:3; 2EpFid 44). Instead of becoming indignant at someone's sin, we should rather try to put ourselves in his place: "Let the custodian mercifully care for him as he would like to be taken care of if he were in a similar position" (EpMin 17). This instruction shows how important Francis thought it was to have compassion in our dealings with our neighbor.

"And thus contrite and confessed, they should receive the Body and Blood of our Lord Jesus Christ with great humility and reverence" (RegNB 20:5). We have already discussed at some length the christological dimension of the Eucharist (cf. above: "We . . . see . . . corporally . . . [the] Body and Blood" p. 65). Here we shall speak only about reception of the Eucharist, that is, holy communion.

As Francis shows in the theological prologue to his *Second Letter to the Faithful* (2EpFid 4-15), the Eucharist contains within It the Passion of Christ, and It draws us on to follow in the footsteps of the Lord so that we may obtain the salvation It brings. Francis invites us to receive communion with pure minds and hearts. While he earnestly recommends that the faithful should receive the Eucharist, he does not say how often they should do so, although we do know that, in the Middle Ages, the norm for reception was about ten times a year (Adm 1:12f.; 1EpFid 1:3; 2:2; 2EpFid 22,63). He also exhorts the friars to go to communion often (RegNB 20:5; EpOrd 19), and courteously calls upon the city authorities to receive also: "I firmly advise you, my lords, to put aside all care and preoccupation and receive with joy the most holy Body and the most holy Blood of our Lord Jesus Christ in holy remembrance of Him" (EpRect 6). To show why we should receive the Eucharist, he quotes our Lord's words indirectly: "He who does not eat His flesh and does not drink His blood cannot enter the Kingdom of God," a strange combination of quotations from St. John's Gospel, one on the Eucharist (Jn 6:53), and the other on baptism (Jn 3:5). But he also quotes our Lord's words directly as a positive reason for receiving communion: "Whoever eats my flesh and drinks my blood has eternal life" (Jn 6:54; RegNB 20:5; Adm 1:11).

The Eucharist, then, is at once a thanksgiving, a memorial, a source of life, and It grants entrance to the Kingdom; and we can also apply to the Eucharist Francis's words in his *Prayer Inspired by the Our Father*, like "our daily bread." It is a "memory and understanding and reverence of the love which our Lord Jesus Christ had for us" (ExpPat 6).

To receive the sacrament "with great humility and veneration," as St. Paul directs (1Cor 11:27-29), a quotation to which Francis frequently refers (Adm 1:13; 2EpFid 27; EpOrd 16,19), we must examine and test ourselves. Otherwise,

> a person despises, defiles and tramples on the Lamb of God when, as the Apostle says, he does not recognize and discern the holy bread of Christ from other foods or actions or eats it unworthily or indeed, even if he were worthy, eats it unthinkingly or without the proper dispositions (EpOrd 19).

To eat worthily means to acknowledge our sins, to approach the Eucharist "contrite and confessed" (RegNB 20:5), "holding back nothing of [ourselves] for [ourselves] so that He who gives Himself totally to [us] may receive [us] totally" (EpOrd 29). The attitude which Francis requires of priests celebrating Mass (EpOrd 14-16) applies equally to those who receive communion: "being pure . . . , with a holy and pure intention . . . , [with] every wish . . . directed to God . . . to please only the most high Lord" (EpOrd 14-16). But Francis's original contribution is the role which he assigns to the Holy Spirit in the reception of the sacrament:

It is the Spirit of the Lord, who lives in His faithful, who receives the most holy Body and Blood of the Lord. All others who do not share in this same Spirit and who presume to receive Him, eat and drink judgment to themselves (1Cor 11:29; Adm 1:12f.).

Living "as Catholics" certainly means receiving the sacraments, but it also requires us

to visit churches frequently and venerate and show respect for the clergy, not so much for them personally if they are sinners, but by reason of their office and their administration of the most holy Body and Blood of Christ (2EpFid 33).

In his writings, Francis often speaks about priests (thirty-two times) and clerics (twenty-eight times). The moral and intellectual qualities of some of the clergy left much to be desired (Adm 26:1; Test 7,9). Nevertheless, Francis asked his friars and the faithful at large to have the same faith in them as he had (Test 6; Adm 26:1) and to show them respect, venerating (twice), revering, honoring, loving, and fearing them. The friars were to regard the clergy as their "lords" (RegNB 19:3; Test 8f.), avoiding conflict with them (Test 6,25), and receiving the sacraments from them alone (Adm 26:3; 2EpFid 35; RegNB 20:4; Test 10; EpMin 19). But, on the other hand, he did not hesitate to write a strongly worded letter to the clergy, exhorting them to respect "the most holy Body and Blood of our Lord Jesus Christ and His most holy written words which consecrate His Body" (EpCler 1). Nor did his respect for them prevent him from speaking bluntly to them about the grave neglect, ignorance, and lack of discernment they so often showed towards the celebration and administration of the Eucharist. In addition, he urged them to reform their lives and even threatens them with the judgment of God. He also writes about religious (RegNB 19:3;23:7) and about "theologians and those who minister the most holy divine words" (Test 13), all of whom we must regard as our "lords" (RegNB 19:3) and whom we must "honor and respect . . . as those who minister spirit and life to us" (Test 13).

He gives the reason for his attitude in his *Testament*:

I act in this way since I see nothing corporally of the Most
High Son of God in this world except His most holy Body
and Blood which they receive and which they alone
administer to others (Test 10; 2EpFid 35; Adm 26:3).

He knew that those who had been ordained and duly authorized to
administer the sacraments were the very framework on which the
Church was built, that Church in which alone the true word of God
was preserved and the sacramental mystery of Christ celebrated
for all the faithful. We must remain united with them because
they alone can guarantee us the means of salvation.

"You shall love your neighbor as yourself"
(Mt 22:39)

Francis quotes John the Baptist, "Bear fruits that befit repentance"
(Lk 3:8), twice and goes on to repeat our Lord's commandment to love
our neighbor (Mt 22:39), first explicitly (2EpFid 26f.) and then
implicitly (RegNB 21:3). Love of God and love of neighbor are the
basic expressions of conversion to the new way of life. Love is the
first fruit of "penance," and Francis sums up its twofold demand in
his *Earlier Rule* (21:4): "Give, and it will be given to you" (Lk 6:38),
"Forgive, and you will be forgiven" (Lk 6:37). Love is a positive
movement which consists in giving, while forgiveness means
showing mercy and offering support to our neighbor. Commenting on
the petition in the Our Father, "Thy will be done," Francis equates
this will with the double commandment: "That we may love you
and . . . love our neighbor as ourselves" (ExpPat 5). Besides this
"old" commandment, he also quotes the "new" one: "[The brothers]
should love one another as the Lord says: This is my commandment:
that you love one another as I have loved you" (Jn 15:12; RegNB
11:5). In his *Earlier Rule*, he devotes the whole of chapter 11 to
fraternal relationships, while chapters 4-6 deal with the same
theme, as do eight *Admonitions* (8,9,17,18,20,24,25,26). This subject
was clearly important to him.

We can see clearly how fundamental love is when we read the
beautiful interweaving of Scripture quotations which Francis uses
to describe the Gospel community gathered by and around the Good

Shepherd (RegNB 22:32-40). Because the Lord is in the midst of His brothers to the end and because they are equal among themselves and before their one Father and Lord in heaven, they remain in Him. From the Good Shepherd, who feeds His sheep and gave His life for them, they learn to love one another as He loves them (RegNB 11:5).

From the numerous passages scattered here and there throughout his writings, we know that, for Francis, genuine fraternal love meant approachability and tenderness and a practical love expressed in action and in offering support and forgiveness.

In his two *Rules*, he uses the image of a mother to describe fraternal love:

> Each one should love and care for his brother . . . as a mother loves and cares for her son" (RegNB 9:11); If a mother has such care and love for her son according to the flesh, should not someone love and care for his brother according to the Spirit even more? (RegB 6:8).

He also refers to this motherly tenderness in his *Letter to Brother Leo*: "I speak to you, my son, as a mother"; and he wishes the brothers to show the same tenderness in the way they treat each other (RegB 6:7). He tells them to greet "one another wholeheartedly and lovingly" (RegNB 7:15) and to show kindness to everyone, even to thieves and robbers (RegNB 2:3; 7:14). The *Later Rule* gives a whole list of attitudes reminiscent of the meek in the beatitude (Mt 5:5): "When [the brothers] go about the world . . . , let them be meek, peaceful and unassuming, gentle and humble, speaking courteously to everyone as is becoming" (RegB 3:11). The brothers are to "be modest, by showing meekness towards everyone" (Tit 3:2; RegNB 11:9) and to admit humbly and without any pretense: "I am a useless servant" (Lk 17:10; RegNB 11:3; 23:7).

A benevolent love based on humility must be put into actual practice in daily life: "Let them express the love they have for one another by their deeds, as the Apostle says: Let us love, not in word or speech, but in deed and in truth" (1Jn 3:18; RegNB 11:6). We practice love of neighbor, "charity," by sharing our possessions with others: "Let us give alms since this washes our souls from the stains of our sins and earns us a reward from the Lord" (2EpFid 30f.).

The two references above to mother-love are not concerned with mere sentiment but with concrete, practical contributions. Both passages refer to material needs (e.g. food): "Each [friar] should confidently make known his need to the other, so that he may find what he needs and minister to him" (RegNB 9:10f.). The measure and criterion for supplying these very ordinary but basic needs is the time-worn adage: "Do unto others as you would have them do unto you," the "golden rule," which Francis quotes in its positive and negative forms (Mt 7:12; Tob 4:16; RegNB 4:4f.) and which he uses as many as six times in his writings (RegNB 6:2; 10:1; RegB 6:9; 2EpFid 43; Adm 18:1; EpMin 17). The positive demonstration of love demands that we "rejoice in the good fortunes of others as well as our own" (ExpPat 5; cf. Adm 17:1), that we "love a brother as much when he is sick and cannot repay" us (Adm 24), and even that we do "not wish that [those who impede us] be better Christians" (EpMin 7), out of respect for their individuality.

It is not easy for us to reach these heights of love, especially since we have spontaneous feelings and reactions which we find very difficult to control. With keen psychological insight, Francis advises us: "If there is anyone who does not wish to love [his neighbors] as himself, at least let him do no harm to them but rather do good" (2EpFid 27). He was well aware of the evil, the great evil, that lurks in the human heart. He knew that we all must endure dissension and disappointment and that we inevitably cause each other pain and suffering.

In the *Earlier Rule* (RegNB 11), he enumerates the evils which threaten the friars, but he also suggests the remedies for these evils—remaining silent, regarding ourselves as useless servants, refusing to judge or condemn anyone, reflecting more on our own sins than on the sins of others, bearing with the weaknesses of our neighbor as we would like him to bear with ours, and, especially, forgiving others so that God will forgive us (RegNB 21:5f.). Knowing how difficult it is for us to forgive others truly, he prays: "Whatever we do not forgive perfectly, do you, Lord, enable us to forgive to the full, so that we may truly love our enemies . . . returning no one evil for evil" (Rom 12:17; ExpPat 8).

In his *Letter to a Minister*, Francis gives really astounding counsel:

> There should not be any brother in the world who has sinned, however much he may have possibly sinned, who, after he has looked into your eyes, would go away without having received your mercy, if he is looking for mercy. And if he were not to seek mercy, you should ask him if he wants mercy. And if he should sin thereafter a thousand times before your very eyes, love him more than me so that you may draw him back to the Lord. Always be merciful to brothers such as these (EpMin 9-11).

Francis regarded love of enemies as the very summit of love. In his two *Rules* (RegNB 22:1; RegB 10:10) and in the *Second Letter to the Faithful* (v.38), he quotes our Lord's words on this subject, while he comments on it in Admonition 9 and prays for it in the *Prayer Inspired by the Our Father* (v.8). This is the love which Christ showed when He called His betrayer "friend" (RegNB 22:2), a love which we are invited to practice towards those "who cannot tolerate our very existence and wish to destroy us" (J. Guillet): "Our friends, then, are all those who unjustly inflict upon us trials and ordeals . . . , for we will possess eternal life because of what they bring upon us" (RegNB 22:3f.). Francis places love of enemies first in the Spirit's "holy manner of working" (RegB 10:8-10) and tells us that we can attain it by praying "with a pure heart . . . , humility [and] patience in persecution and weakness." When we have reached this goal, the Spirit teaches us how "to love those who persecute us, find fault with us, or rebuke us, because the Lord says: Love your enemies and pray for those who persecute and slander you." Commenting further on this thought, Francis shows us that we truly love our enemies when we are not upset by the injury they inflict on us, but, out of love of God, are disturbed only by the evil which their sin inflicts on themselves (Adm 9). He must have had personal experience of this since he was able to speak about it with such emotion and even to propose it as an essential part of the Christian life and, indeed, as the summit of that life. We can, then, understand better his prayer: "Lord, enable us to forgive to the full so that we may truly love our enemies and fervently intercede for them before you" (ExpPat 8). And in his *Letter to a Minister*, he goes further and is more specific:

> You should accept as a grace . . . whoever has become an impediment to you, whether they are brothers or others, even if they lay hands on you . . . . And love those who do these things to you. And do not expect anything different from them, unless it is something which the Lord shall have given to you (EpMin 2,5f.).

"Hold back nothing of yourselves for yourselves"
(EpOrd 29)

For Francis, the worst thing that we could do would be to steal what does not belong to us and proudly claim it as our own. Here, he was thinking, not about external possessions, but about our very existence as humans, with all our God-given physical and spiritual gifts and abilities. That would be the ultimate sin, for it would be stealing "the money of [our] Lord God" (Adm 18:2).

Having described the three basic Christian attitudes—a loving relationship with God, life in the Church, and love of neighbor—we can now come to Francis's ideal of "highest poverty." Such poverty consists in three complementary elements—recognizing that everything good belongs to God and must be returned to Him; attributing solely to ourselves the evil in us; and taking upon ourselves the burdens of life "by carrying the cross of our Lord Jesus Christ." We believe that this viewpoint is essential to a correct understanding of Franciscan poverty. Unfortunately, since the great controversies of the thirteenth and fourteenth centuries, and even down to our own times, Francis's idea of poverty has only too often been reduced to its material aspects, renouncing the right to own property, and the restricted used of material things. But Francis's writings present a much more profound, radical view that reaches down to the very roots of our being.

"Let us acknowledge that all good things belong to God" (EpOrd 29)

There is nothing more wonderful and exhilarating than to discover that we bear in us the glorious image of the Lord God (Adm 5:1). What we are and what we can accomplish materially is great and good, and we can rightly rejoice and be proud of it. This is even more true of spiritual things, the most magnificent of which is union with God. But then a temptation creeps in, and we begin to think: "I'm pretty important after all! This and that belong to me! I'm self-sufficient! I'm like God! I *am* God!" In order not to succumb to this temptation, we must relinquish any fatuous claim to our good qualities and gifts, which we do not own. We should remember Francis's uncompromising words on this subject in his *Earlier Rule*:

> Let us refer all good to the most high and supreme Lord God, and acknowledge that every good is His, and thank Him for everything, He from whom all good things come (RegNB 17:17).

In these few lines, he says everything. God alone is good, the Source of all good (Lk 18:18f.), good which He spreads everywhere and concentrates in us humans; and we must always acknowledge that everything good belongs solely to God and comes from His generosity.

But mere acknowledgment is not enough. We must hasten to return God's gifts to him, restore them to Him to whom they belong. This voluntary returning of God's gifts implies that we acknowledge, not only the value of those gifts, but especially His infinite, undeserved generosity, the result of His love for us. Our acknowledgment of our indebtedness then becomes a "thanksgiving," a formula which Francis uses fifteen times in his writings and in which he himself acknowledges and returns the gift to the Giver, thus celebrating His love for us.

The *Admonitions*, too, insist on our duty to refer everything back to God—spiritual knowledge of the Scriptures (Adm 7:4), the ability to remain peaceful in the midst of evil (Adm 11:4), in fact, literally, *everything*. Truly,

> ... blessed is the servant who attributes every good to the Lord God, for he who holds back something for himself, hides within himself the money of his Lord God (Mt 25:18), and that which he thought he had shall be taken away from him (Lk 8:18; Adm 18:2).

And when we have restored everything to God, He gives it all back to us: receiving and giving are demonstrations of love inspired by a dependence that is not humiliating. But if we are foolish enough to keep anything back for ourselves, we find that we are left wretched and stripped of everything. Real, profound poverty is having nothing of our own and regarding everything as a gift from God: "Hold back nothing of yourselves for yourselves so that He who gives Himself totally to you may receive you totally" (EpOrd 29). We must give up self, renounce any claim to ownership of whatever we are or have if we wish to be acceptable to God, because God Himself followed the way of poverty by giving Himself to and for us. As Francis used to pray at the conclusion of his *Office of the Passion*, "Let us bless the Lord, the living and true God; to Him let us always render praise, glory, honor, blessing and *every good*. Amen. Amen. So be it. So be it."

It would be difficult to find better words to express our thanks to God. Real thanksgiving is not a slow, painful renunciation of everything but rather a cry of joy acknowledging the good things we have received and rejoicing in the Source from whom they come, from God, who is love.

"Nothing belongs to us except our vices and sins"
(RegNB 17:7)

Francis counsels us "not [to] keep anything for [ourselves], rendering to Caesar what is Caesar's and to God what is God's" (Adm 11:4). But there is one exception to this total stripping of self: "We should be firmly convinced that nothing belongs to us except our vices and sins" (RegNB 17:7). Anything good that we have or do, no matter how personal it is, comes to us from God, and we are only administrators of that good, as it were. Yet something does belong to us alone—"our vices and sins." By presenting the negative side of our humanity, we have demonstrated from Francis's writings that he knew and described clinically the nature of the evil and wretchedness in our lives. For him, evil does not come from God or the devil or our neighbor (Adm 10:1). He insists strenuously that we are responsible for Original Sin: "Through our own fault we have fallen" (RegNB 23:2), so that it is "through our own fault" that we are so wretched (2EpFid 46; RegNB 22:6). And since we are "miserable and contemptible" beyond words (2EpFid 46), we deserve only hatred: "We must hate our bodies with their vices and sins" (2EpFid 37; RegNB 22:6; 1EpFid 12); "Let us hold ourselves in contempt and scorn" (2EpFid 46). We are truly poor when we "hate" ourselves (cf. Adm 14:4), and Francis reminds us six times in his writings of this duty to "hate" ourselves. The expression "to hate oneself" comes from the Gospels (Lk 14:26; Jn 12:25) and has often been commented upon at great length. Yet Francis's insistence on the point seems excessive, the more so since he never explains precisely what hatred of self entails psychologically or spiritually.

First, however, let us clear up a possible misunderstanding. As we have seen before, when Francis speaks about the body, he is not referring to the physical body but to that which is the source of evil and sin within us, that is, our whole personality in so far as "we are . . . opposed to good but prompt and willing to embrace evil" (RegNB 22:6). But what does it mean to "hate" this aspect of ourselves? Admonition 12 gives the outline of an answer when it says that:

> A servant of God may be recognized as possessing the Spirit of the Lord in this way: the flesh does not pride itself when the Lord performs some good through him . . . , rather he considers himself the more worthless in his own eyes and esteems himself less than all others.

This can be called "humility" but certainly not "hatred" of oneself.

When we examine the general trend of Francis's writings, we can reach a tentative conclusion about the spiritual and psychological meaning of this "hatred of self" to which he returns so often. As we have said before, we are aware first of the gifts which God showers on us and which we are called upon to acknowledge and return in an act of thanksgiving. But when we discover the other aspect of our being, the source of evil in our hearts, from which come "vices and sins," how are we to deal with it? Are we to blame God or other people or circumstances? We are tempted to do so, but giving in to that temptation solves nothing:

> The real enemy . . . is the body through which [we] sin. Therefore, blessed is that servant who, having such an

enemy in his power, will always . . . wisely guard himself
against him (Adm 10:2f.).

Having that enemy in our power and being on our guard against i t
consists, first, in recognizing that we have within us a mysterious
open wound that is part of our condition as weak, limited creatures.
This wound causes us to suffer, and we add to this suffering by
constantly irritating the wound and making it worse by our conduct.
Unless we are masochists, we cannot like or take pleasure in this
state of affairs. But can we "hate" our condition in the psychological meaning of that term? If by hating we mean recoiling from,
detesting, rejecting, or despising it, we must not do so because this
would be self-destructive: in spite of everything, we would then be
destroying a part of what we are. "Hating our bodies," then, is
acknowledging the evil that is in us and bearing with it as we
would with an illness. We try to cure it but we know that we shall
never succeed fully. And we cry out to God in our distress, patiently
waiting for the day when the Divine Physician will free us, once
and for all, at the time of our death and resurrection.

Although Francis uses harsh, uncompromising words, he is
really asking us to be patient and merciful with ourselves because
how can we be prepared to forgive and be merciful to others if we
cannot do so with ourselves? For the rest, it is striking to see that,
at least three times, Francis associates hatred of self with love of
enemies (RegNB 22:1,5; 2EpFid 37f.; Adm 14:4), as if the two
attitudes are closely linked, the one implying the other. Perhaps
by this association, Francis wants to say that we should be ready to
bear with the hateful part of ourselves in the same way that we
force ourselves to love someone who is totally repulsive to us. In
Admonition 5, he reaches the same conclusion. Having excluded all
the good things of which we could be proud but which do not belong
to us, he goes on to quote St. Paul: "I will not boast, except of my
weaknesses" (2Cor 12:5), weaknesses that are not only human
limitations but also "our body with its vices and sins."

"Bearing daily the holy cross of our Lord Jesus Christ" (Adm 5:8)

Francis's biographers depict his spiritual journey as joyful, light-hearted, filled with poetry and song. To them, he is a merry troubadour, dancing, singing, and playing music, if only on a couple of pieces of wood. But his writings show a more somber side of his character, one that is marked by his experience of the cross: "We can glory in our infirmities (cf. 2Cor 12:5) and bearing daily the holy cross of our Lord Jesus Christ" (Adm 5:8; cf. Lk 14:27). In dramatic words, he tells us precisely what bearing the cross of Christ means:

> We must rejoice when we . . . fall into various trials (Jas 1:2) and endure every sort of anguish of soul and body or ordeals in this world for the sake of eternal life (RegNB 17:8).

Elsewhere he assures us that

> our friends are those who unjustly inflict upon us trials and ordeals, shame and injuries, sorrows and torments, martyr-dom and death; we must love them greatly for we will possess eternal life because of what they bring upon us (RegNB 22:3f.).

His division of "trials and ordeals" into three pairs was not haphazard but indicated a gradation of suffering—psychological trials, verbal and physical abuse, followed finally by torture and death. While we do not know to what extent these descriptions were based on actual experience, we do know that Francis and the friars whom he was addressing had been in similar situations. Admonition 6 tells us that the path of suffering was first chosen and followed by

> the Good Shepherd who suffered the passion of the cross to save His sheep. The sheep of the Lord followed Him in tribulation and persecution, in insult and hunger, in infirmity and temptation, and in everything else, and they have received everlasting life from the Lord because of these things.

When speaking about going among nonbelievers, Francis reminds the friars—and us as well—that

> all the brothers, wherever they may be, should remember that they gave themselves and abandoned their bodies to the Lord Jesus Christ. And for love of Him, they must make themselves vulnerable to their enemies, both visible and invisible (RegNB 16:10f.).

He then goes on to give nine quotations from the New Testament, all referring to the way we should conduct ourselves in times of persecution and urging us to endure and persevere (RegNB 16:11-21).

Francis's description of "true and perfect joy"—to which we shall return later—evokes the same somber atmosphere of suffering to be endured in patience and without being disturbed by it. Clearly, then, he believed that our human condition entails suffering from which none of us can escape and which we must accept by following in the footsteps of Christ crucified.

The texts give a number of concrete examples of the sufferings which test us—submitting to everyone, rejection by those close to us, sickness and death. Francis then invites the friars to be "the lesser ones [minores] and subject to all" wherever they are working (RegNB 7:2), and he states that this was the way the friars acted from the beginning (Test 19). This attitude caused them to suffer humiliations and violence, as we can see from the *Earlier Rule* (RegNB 14:4f.), which urges them not to resist evil (Lk 6:29). And this was the way they were to act at all times and not only among nonbelievers, where he told them that they should "be subject to every human creature for God's sake" (1Pet 2:13; RegNB 16:6). They might be evicted from their dwellings (RegNB 7:13) or persecuted by priests, but, instead of protesting or seeking protection from Rome, they were to "flee into another country to do penance" (Test 26).

Francis describes the most profound form of this submission to others in a mysterious text in which he speaks about the effects of obedience, which subdues our fleshly egos and submits them to the Spirit and our neighbors:

> Holy Obedience destroys every wish of the body and of the flesh and binds its mortified body to obedience to the Spirit

and to obedience to one's brother; and the person who possesses her is subject and submissive to all persons in the world and not to man only but even to all beasts and wild animals, so that they may do whatever they want with him, inasmuch as it has been given to them from above by the Lord (SalVirt 14-18).

Instead of humbling and destroying us, the trial of *submission* leads us to a kind of self-abandonment, a letting go of self, a sort of unruffled calm, the *apatheia* or *ataraxia* of the ancient philosophers.

Rejection by those close to us (by the other friars, in the text) is an even greater trial. Unlike the over-long, over-poetic account in the *Fioretti*, the original version of *True and Perfect Joy* dramatizes and crystallizes this rejection. "True joy . . . , true virtue and the salvation of the soul" do not consist in the success of the movement which Francis began, success such as having "all the prelates beyond the mountains" and even the kings of France and England enter the Order, or in the conversion of all nonbelievers, or in being given the gift of healing and performing miracles. In what does true joy consist, then? Giving himself as an example, Francis describes a dark stormy night in the depth of winter, when he is cold and covered in mud, his legs bleeding from the icicles that have formed on the hem of his habit. He arrives at a friary but no one answers although he keeps knocking at the door for a long time. Finally, the doorkeeper does answer and, although he recognizes Francis, tells him roughly that it is very late, adding: "Go away, you are a simple and a stupid person . . . ; we have no need of you . . . Go to the Crosiers's place [with the lepers]!"

The very thought of such a callous rejection saddens and revolts us because it would be a grave breach of fraternal love and a total turning away from a fellow human being. We would expect almost any reaction to this treatment except joy, but that is exactly what Francis suggests: "I tell you this: if I had patience and did not become upset, there would be true joy in this and the salvation of the soul" (VPLaet). He does not tell us here the source of such patience and joy, but in Admonition 15 he states that it is confidence in the "love of our Lord Jesus Christ" which empowers us to preserve peace of mind and joy in all our sufferings in this world.

Illness is another kind of trial which allows us to share in Christ's cross. Francis himself suffered this thorn in his flesh almost all his life. Besides the descriptions given by his biographers, he himself alludes to his state of health four times in his writings (2EpFid 3; EpOrd 39; Test 29), most graphically when he tells us that: "because of my weakness and the pain of my sickness, I am not strong enough to speak" (TestSen). In both *Rules*, he devotes passages and even a whole chapter to the sick friars (RegNB 10; RegB 6:9; 10:2), while, in many other texts, he mentions in passing "the healthy and the sick" (RegNB 23:7), "the sick and the lepers" (RegNB 9:2), those who follow the Lord "in infirmity and temptation" (Adm 6:2) and who "bear infirmity and tribulation" (CantSol). In chapter 10 of the *Earlier Rule*, he urges all the sick friars—and others:

> I beg the sick brother to give thanks to the Creator for everything; and whatever the Lord wills for him, he should desire to be that, whether healthy or sick, since all those whom God has predestined for everlasting life He instructs by means of the afflictions of punishment and sickness and the spirit of repentance (RegNB 10:5).

This exhortation takes into account all the burdens and difficulties of illness, the mental pain of anxiety and depression as well as the physical suffering. The rest of the text considers also the thoughts that may assail someone who is sick and who becomes "disturbed or . . . angry at God or his brothers . . . , persistently ask[ing] for medicines with a great desire to free the flesh" (RegNB 10:4). In his *Canticle of Brother Sun*, Francis speaks from personal experience when he exclaims: "Praise be you, my Lord, through those who . . . bear infirmity and tribulation. Blessed are those who endure in peace" (CantSol 10f.). He expresses the same thoughts in his *Canticle of Exhortation to St. Clare and Her Sisters* (CantExh). His words were not mere consoling platitudes but came from the heart of one who knew what sickness meant. He was gravely ill then and had borne an almost intolerable burden of suffering for a long time. Yet he had found within himself and especially in God the strength to endure. He had reached the stage where he was almost indifferent to his afflictions and was even able to thank God for them; and he urged his brothers to do the same and to carry the cross "as the Lord wishes," as he mentions elsewhere.

Finally, our last and cruelest enemy is *death* (1Cor 15:26), which seems to put an end to everything and which, no matter how we view it, remains "the unknown horror" (Marie Noël). The theme of death has a place of some importance in Francis's writings, in which the words "death" and "to die" occur frequently (fifteen and twenty-one times respectively), especially in those texts addressed to all Christians (1EpFid 2:14-16; 2EpFid 71f.,81-85; EpRect 2-5; RegNB 21:3,7f.; CantSol 12f.). In his *Office of the Passion*, Francis depicts Christ as speaking about His death (OffPass, Ps 2:10; 6:10; 13:4). Led "into the dust of death," Christ has risen (Ps 6:11), no more to die (EpOrd 22), and it is by the cross, blood, and death of the Son that the Father saves us (RegNB 23:3). The death of the body, our last horizon on earth, also has a place in Francis's vision of life: "the flesh which is soon to die" (RegNB 10:4); "we will soon die" (RegNB 21:30); "death approaches" (1EpFid 2:16); "Death, from whom no living man can escape" (CantSol 12); "bitter death" (1EpFid 2:14). We travel towards this horizon, not knowing when or where we shall reach it (2EpFid 71). Death is decisive, final, a time when we shall be stripped of what we think we have: "every talent, every power and knowledge and wisdom," every possession, "will be taken away from [us]" (1EpFid 2:16). Therefore, this fate that awaits us should make us stop and think: "Pause and reflect, for the day of death is approaching. I beg you, therefore, with all possible respect, not to forget the Lord or turn away from His commandments" (EpRect 2f.).

When we face up to this challenge and change our lives, death loses the worst of its terror and becomes for us a door to life, so much so that Francis could call it "our Sister Bodily Death" (CantSol 12). He declares: "Blessed are those whom death will find in your most holy will, for the second death—that is, rejection by God—shall do them no harm" (CantSol 13). Such a happy death, especially when it shares in Christ's death through martyrdom, is in complete contrast to the death of the sinner, which Francis depicts in dark, dramatic colors (2EpFid 70-85).

In these texts, Francis presents death as a solemn, even touching, event but also as a reckoning that is painful, decisive, and mysterious. When he praised the Lord for "our Sister Bodily Death," he had overcome his natural reaction of fear and abhorrence. But, while he had thus come to terms with death, he had not changed its nature or turned it into something banal and unremarkable. Instead, he had taught himself not to fear the threatening, incomprehensible passage of death. He invites us rather to look to the hope that, at the other end of that dark, narrow tunnel, there awaits us, not total extinction nor any other horror but, rather, "the Kingdom . . . prepared . . . from the beginning of the world" (RegNB 23:4).

"Following in the footsteps of our Lord Jesus Christ"

In various forms, St. Peter's admonition: "You should follow in [Christ's] steps" (1Pet 2:21) occurs five times in Francis's writings (RegNB 1:1; 22:2; 2EpFid 13; EpOrd 51; EpLeo 3). For Francis, these words apparently summed up the whole aim of the Christian life. It is often said that following Christ, *sequela Christi*, is also the essence of the *Franciscan* life, an assessment that seems to be justified by the important place the phrase occupies in Francis's works. Let us see what "following Christ" means precisely.

In his epistle, St. Peter was not speaking about sharing in Christ's earthly life of poverty and itinerant preaching but rather about "endur[ing] pain while suffering unjustly" as Christ did, for He had "committed no sin" (1Pet 2:19,22). The two places where Francis uses St. Peter's phrase explicitly are both in the same line of thought. The expression "following in Christ's footsteps" in the *Second Letter to the Faithful* (v.13) refers to Christ's whole life, but especially to His Passion, His giving Himself to the Father and to us by surrendering His will to His Father and in the Eucharist. And in the *Earlier Rule* (22:1-4), "following in Christ's footsteps" means "loving our enemies," as Christ did when He "called His betrayer "friend" and gave Himself willingly to those who crucified Him."

If we take St. Peter's text to include all chapter 22 of the *Earlier Rule*, then following in Christ's footsteps means extending our love of neighbor to include our enemies (vv.1-4), dying to our sinful, egotistical selves (vv.5-8), and, above all, opening our hearts to the Lord (vv.9-41). These two places in which Francis quotes St. Peter give us a key to interpreting the other texts where his application of the quotation is less explicit.

Thus, in the *Letter to the Entire Order* (v.51), "to follow in the footsteps of your beloved Son" undoubtedly refers to the same basic themes (the Passion and sufferings of Christ) but here the outcome is a happy one, as "we make our way to you, Most High." Similarly, the *Earlier Rule* states formally that the friars' way of life is "to follow . . . in the footsteps of our Lord Jesus Christ" (RegNB 1:1). The four quotations from the Gospel that come next in the *Rule* refer to selling everything and giving the money to the poor, renouncing self, carrying the cross, breaking family ties, and, finally, receiving in return a hundredfold and eternal life (RegNB 1:1-5). Therefore, following Christ makes demands upon us, especially inner demands, but it leads to the life and glory promised in Christ's prayer: "I desire that they also, whom you have given me, may be with me where I am, to behold [your] glory" (Jn 17:24; RegNB 22:55). We should understand in the same sense such references as "to follow in His footsteps and His poverty," and "I . . . wish to follow the life and poverty of our most high Lord Jesus Christ" (UltVol), which make poverty one of the main elements of Christ's life.

It is plain from these texts that "following in Christ's footsteps" does not mean imitating Christ's earthly life in detail. Instead, it indicates "following" or accepting the whole Gospel, its revelations, promises and various demands without singling out any one of them. But if one element were to be selected, it would be the one proposed by St. Peter (1Pet 2:21), that is, willingly and patiently sharing in the mystery of the Lord's blessed Passion. Then, instead of being seen as a mysticism of earthly poverty, "following Christ" would be a mysticism of His Passion, leading to final glory with Him. "Following in Christ's footsteps," therefore, means living according to all the demands of the Gospel, including suffering and death, and looking towards the rewards promised in that Gospel.

Francis proposes "following Christ" as a program of life to all Christians (2EpFid) as well as to the friars (RegNB 22). In the Middle Ages, "following in Christ's footsteps" was taken to mean living the common life in poverty and itinerant preaching; and even still efforts are made to reconcile this with what Francis says in his writings. But an analysis of the texts shows that they contain much more and that they are focused on sharing in Christ's painful Passion and glorious Resurrection. In this sense, "following Christ" means the whole Christian life and summarizes very well the spiritual journey we have been describing.

The Franciscan "Beatitudes"

The path we have to follow is not an easy one. We must take everything good in us and give it back to God; we must acknowledge the evil that alone belongs to us; and we must embark on a journey that demands complete self-abnegation. How can we do it? Francis gives us the answer in a phrase he uses five times: "with patience and humility." Trials show us whether or not we have the correct attitude:

> The servant of God cannot know how much patience and humility he has within himself as long as everything goes well with him. But when the time comes in which those who should do him justice do quite the opposite to him, he has only as much patience and humility as he has on that occasion and no more (Adm 13).

Patience and humility go together as a pair (SalVirt 2) and are fruits of the Spirit (RegNB 17:15): we have greatest need of them in persecution and illness (RegB 10:9) as well as in fraternal relationships (2EpFid 44), so that we do not become upset (VPLaet 5). Patience is the capacity to endure hardship, to carry on and not allow ourselves to give up or be overcome in difficult situations. It must be accompanied by humility, which helps us to see ourselves as we really are, weak, uncertain. and threatened, but also unique and of infinite value. Admonition 19 describes true humility well and shows how hard it is:

> Blessed is the servant who esteems himself no better when he is praised and exalted by people than when he is

considered worthless, simple and despicable: for what a man is before God, that he is and nothing more.

Although we are made in God's likeness, we are also miserable sinners.

To patience and humility, we must add joy. Francis uses five terms to describe this state of mind: "joy, joyful" (*laetitia, laetor*—twenty times), "exultation" (fifteen times), "rejoicing" (*gaudium, gaudere*—fourteen times), and two unusual words "gladness" (*iucunditas*) and "cheerful" (*hilaris*). Most of these appear in his *Office of the Passion*, which celebrates the victory of Christ crucified. Speaking about the place of joy in life, Francis puts the brothers on their guard against appearing "outwardly sad and like gloomy hypocrites" and tells them, instead, to "show that they are joyful in the Lord and cheerful and truly gracious" (RegNB 7:16).

In fact, Francis calls God "joy": "You are joy: you are our hope and joy" (LaudDei 4), and Christ gives His joy to His disciples (Jn 17:13; RegNB 22:46). This "joy in the Lord" is experienced in meditating on "the most holy words and deeds of the Lord," in which we find "the joy and gladness" by means of which we can lead others to the love of God (Adm 20). Joy accompanies poverty (Adm 27:3). Francis calls Brother Fire *iocundo*, "joyful, merry, playful" (CantSol 8) but does not say what joy consists in: yet can anyone else do so? When he speaks about "true and perfect joy" (VPLaet), he emphasizes its paradoxical nature, the fact that it is joy that sustains and encourages us to endure in peace when everything seems lost. He equates joy with "true virtue and the salvation of the soul" (VPLaet 15). "We must rejoice when we . . . fall into various trials" (RegNB 17:8), or "when [we] live among people who are . . . looked down upon" (RegNB 9:2), as we are urged to do in the beatitude on those who suffer persecution (Lk 6:23; RegNB 16:6).

Although the path of the Christian life seems difficult, those who embark on it are strangely joyful. Fifteen of the twenty-eight *Admonitions* begin with the exclamation "Blessed!" that is, "Happy!" (Adms 13-26,28). Francis comments on four of St. Matthew's beatitudes: the poor in spirit (Adm 14), the peacemakers (Adms 13,15), the pure of heart (Adm 16) and the persecuted (RegNB 16; 12:15; RegB 10:11). St. Matthew seems to reserve for the next life the happiness which the beatitudes promise; but Francis sees this happiness already at work in those who accept the demands and the promises of the Gospel, an often paradoxical situation. Thus, Francis proclaims:

> . . . Happy is that servant who, having such an enemy [his body] in his power will always . . . wisely guard himself against him (Adm 10). Happy is he who does not keep anything for himself, rendering to . . . God what is God's (Adm 11). Happy are the peacemakers. . . . The servant of God . . . knows . . . he has only as much patience and humility [as he shows] when those who should do him justice do quite the opposite to him (Adm 13:1-2). Happy are the poor in spirit . . . who hate [themselves] and love those who strike [them] on the cheek (Adm 14). Happy are the peacemakers [who] . . . preserve peace of mind and body . . . despite what they suffer in this world (Adm 15). Happy are the pure of heart . . . who despise the things of earth and seek the things of heaven and who never cease to adore and behold the Lord God, living and true (Adm 16). Happy is that servant who does not pride himself on the good that the Lord says or does through him any more than on what He says or does through another (Adm 17). Happy is the person who bears with his neighbor in his weakness . . . and attributes every good to the Lord God (Adm 18). Happy is the servant who esteems himself no better . . . [than] what [he is] before God . . . and nothing more . . . , [and who] always desires to be under the feet of others (Adm 19). Happy is [he] who takes no pleasure and joy except in the most holy words and deeds of the Lord (Adm 20). Happy is the servant who, when he speaks, does not reveal everything about himself . . . but wisely weighs what he should say (Adm 21). Happy is the servant who would accept correction. . . . Happy is the servant who, when he is rebuked, quietly agrees. . . . Happy is the servant who is not quick to excuse himself . . . , even though he did not commit any fault (Adm 22). Happy is the servant who is found to be as humble among his subjects as he would be among his masters (Adm 23). Happy is the servant who would love his brother as much when he is sick and cannot repay him as he would when he is well and

can repay him (Adm 24). Happy is the servant who would love and respect his brother as much when he is far from him as he would when he is with him; and who would not say anything behind his back which in charity he would not say to his face (Adm 25). Happy is the servant who has faith in the clergy . . . of the Roman Church (Adm 26). Happy is that servant who keeps the secrets of the Lord in his heart . . . and does not desire to reveal them to others (Adm 28). Happy are you when people shall hate you and malign and persecute you and drive you out" (RegNB 16:15; RegB 10:11).

This is a strange form of happiness! Being happy normally means feeling contented, secure, and inwardly calm, in a state of peace and joy. But the situations which Francis describes as happy are mostly those which make us suffer or, at least, make difficult demands on us. Francis's "beatitudes," like those in the Gospel, presuppose the presence of a mysterious state of soul, a state of "humility and patience and the pure and simple and true peace of the spiritual person" (RegNB 17:15), the basis of a joy that nothing can destroy.

Two beautifully poetic texts, Admonition 27 and the *Salutation of the Virtues*, celebrate the reign of the virtues in our hearts, where they have taken up their abode. Francis constantly refers to the virtues in pairs (Adm 17—five times: SalVirt—three times). Charity is accompanied by wisdom, patience goes hand-in-hand with humility, poverty with joy, inner peace with meditation, and mercy with discernment, while "the fear of the Lord . . . guard[s] the house" so that "the enemy cannot enter" (Adm 27). This admonition, which can be regarded as belonging to the monastic contemplative tradition, associates the different virtues, makes them complementary, and thus balances them, one with the other. Charity enlightens us, gives us a desire for God and removes servile fear and ignorance. Patience and humility exclude anger and mental turmoil. Poverty, strangely associated with joy, eliminates all covetousness and avarice. Peace and meditation are opposed to anxiety and dissipation. Mercy, joined with discernment, removes "excess" and "hardness of heart." These are vignettes that breathe peace, harmony, and beauty and depict a state which can be reached by "those who preserve peace of mind and body for love of our Lord Jesus Christ, despite what they suffer in this world" (Adm 15).

The *Salutation of the Virtues* takes another approach, giving only three pairs of virtues but describing their "operations" at greater length, especially those of obedience. As poetry, the *Salutation* is more carefully crafted and richer in imagery than Admonition 27 and is really a courtly form of greeting. It begins with the word *Ave!*, "Hail!," addressed to the first virtue, "Queen Wisdom," who is accompanied by her "sister, holy pure Simplicity." Next come "holy Poverty" and her "sister, holy Humility," then "holy Charity" and her "sister, holy Obedience." Four of these six virtues are named in Admonition 27; simplicity and obedience are added here. These personified virtues "proceed" from God and not from us, for we must "die" before we can possess them (v.5). They are so intertwined with each other that, when we possess any one of them, we possess them all; and when one of them is "offended," all disappear. Each one "destroys" (*confundit*), that is, disperses or reduces to nothing whatever is contrary to it. "Wisdom destroys Satan and all his subtlety," while "Simplicity destroys all the wisdom of the world and the wisdom of the body." Humility banishes pride, and "Charity destroys every temptation of the devil and of the flesh and every carnal fear." Finally, "Obedience destroys every wish of the body and of the flesh and binds its mortified body to obedience to the Spirit and to obedience of one's brother and . . . to all persons in the world and . . . even to all beasts and wild animals."

Francis believed that, despite all the dangers, obstacles, and even the afflictions we encounter in this life, we can achieve here on earth a state of serenity reminiscent of that advocated by the oriental sages and well known in the monastic tradition of the Fathers of the Desert. He indicated this by choosing wisdom as the "Queen" of the virtues. This wisdom, however, is not merely the human virtue raised to the level of a unifying, balancing power. Instead, when combined with the fear and love of God, it is a kind of divine influence and attribute, as he tells us in his *Earlier Rule*:

> Above all things, [the Spirit of the Lord] always longs for
> the divine *fear* and the divine *wisdom* and all the divine

love of the Father, and of the Son, and of the Holy Spirit
(RegNB 17:16).

Christ alone, "who is the true wisdom of the Father" (1EpFid 2:8)
becomes the essential wisdom of those who welcome Him.

A New View of the World

We have arrived at this point, animated, not by the spirit of the
flesh, but by "the holy virtues, which, through the grace and light
of the Holy Spirit are poured into the hearts of the faithful"
(SalBMV 6). We can now look at the world around us with new
eyes. Admonition 16, on "purity of heart," would seem to require us
to "despise the things of earth." But we should, rather, translate
the Latin *terrena despicere* as "to look upon the things of earth
from on high, from the point of view of eternity." Indeed, one of
Francis's best known writings, his *Canticle of Brother Sun*, is far
from asking us to despise the world around us. On the contrary, in it
Francis turns our eyes towards the beauty of material creation. His
insight into the painful and apparently meaningless events of this
world, such as suffering and death, transfigures them.

The *Canticle* does not really extol creation but is a song of
praise to the "Most High [whose name] no man is worthy to
mention" (CantSol 1). To Him alone belongs praise by and for all
the creatures which reflect some of His dazzling glory. Looking at
creation with eyes purified by suffering and tears, Francis
composed this canticle while gravely ill and almost blind and
after he had endured a dark night of the soul. He saw and named
the basic elements of God's world, the day with its triumphant sun;
the night with its shining moon and stars; the ever-moving wind;
water, humble and useful; and the earth with its flowers and fruits
and herbs. He groups these six elements in couples, with masculine
and feminine alternating, and calls each "brother," "sister," or
"mother," according to the symbolic gender he allots to it. He was
the first to perceive a kind of blood relationship between
inanimate elements in nature. In fact, the titles "brother," "sister"
and "mother," besides expressing a tender family feeling, imply
that they are all composed of the same material and come from the
same Source.

Francis presents these related creatures as parts of a harmonious whole. In the first place comes "Sir Brother Sun," the pre-eminent symbol of God's glory because he is "beautiful and radiant with great splendor," giving us daytime and light. The moon and the stars are feminine, for they are "clear and precious and beautiful." While Francis does not use any adjectives to describe the wind, he does stress its influence on "the air, cloudy and serene, and every kind of weather." Sister Water is a humble maiden, "precious and chaste." Beautiful Brother Fire lights up the night with a joy that shows how robust and strong he is. Our Sister Earth is a loving mother who feeds us and supplies us with fruits and herbs and flowers.

After marveling at the beauty of creation, Francis turns to us humans, not to praise our beauty and strength but to show that we have been wounded by sin, afflicted with "infirmity and tribulation," and destined to feel the pangs of death. In contrast and opposition to the harmony of nature, Francis depicts our humanity in the somber tones of suffering and inevitable death. Nevertheless, he praises the Lord even for all this because, knowing that He loves us, we can bear illness and trials with peaceful minds. Francis calls death by the tender, loving name of "Sister" and portrays it as having been subdued and even as gentle. Because none of us can escape death, we must accept its mysterious obscurity and abandon ourselves to God's will in its regard. That is why, immediately after praising God for His creation, we can go on to extol Him by accepting our mortality and can look to Him in hope because, then, "the second death shall do [us] no harm."

Francis achieved the unity of this canticle and its harmony of contrasts by associating and reconciling the two facets of reality. He shows that, while God is readily seen in the order and beauty of the world, He is also present in our sufferings and death when we accept them from His hands. We look with wonder and gratitude, not only at the beautiful order of creation, but also at our pain, whose hidden meaning we learn to sense and accept.

The spiritual journey which Francis proposes takes into account our complex humanity and requires our humble, patient acceptance of what we are. We have been showered with countless extraordinary gifts, which we must acknowledge but without appropriating them. We must also recognize our faults and failings and accept them as patiently as we can, since life is not all good but has negative elements in it, too. When we acknowledge this double-edged situation, we can enter the mystery of Christ's cross and follow in His footsteps. On this path we shall gradually find that, for us, as for Francis, "what seemed bitter [will be] changed into sweetness of soul and body" (Test 3). The stern demands of death to self, of inner self-renunciation, of openness and service to our neighbor, will paradoxically bring us the joy of the beatitudes and the peaceful rule of the virtues of poverty, purity of heart, peace and, above all, wisdom, knowledge of God, and the desire for Him. That is what Francis has to teach us about our "human condition."

Chapter 6

Particular Vocations

In the preceding chapters, we have dealt with people in general—what they are, what they do, and what they are called to become. We were speaking in generalities, about things that are applicable to all Christians. Although some of the passages we examined were addressed to particular categories of people, they were also applicable to all believers and were presented in that perspective.

However, parts of Francis's writings refer to specific vocations—the "penitents," the Friars Minor, and the sisters at San Damiano. The two versions of the *Letter to the Faithful* are addressed to "penitents." The *Earlier* and *Later Rules*, the *Rule for Hermitages*, the *Testament*, the *Testament of Siena,* and the *Letter to the Entire Order* describe and legislate for the lives of the friars, while three brief documents refer to the sisters at San Damiano.

In this chapter, we shall examine each of these vocations, keeping in mind that what we have said above about Christians in general is valid also for them and does not need to be repeated. We wish only to show what is special to each of the vocations in question, remembering that the basic elements, the demands and promises of the Gospel, are always applicable and are the same for everyone.

The Way of the "Penitents"

Why do we speak about "penitents" when this word does not appear anywhere in Francis's writings? The *Second Letter to the Faithful* does not prescribe a way of life meant for the laity alone, but is addressed to "all Christian religious: clergy and laity, men and women." No doubt it would have been clearer if Francis had written to "all Christians living in the world." Instead, he used the term "religious" to indicate the group for whom he wrote the letter; and to understand fully the meaning he attached to this word, "religious" (which he repeats in v.36), we must analyze what he meant by "penance."

This term appears no less than twenty-eight times in his writings. In eighteen cases, it indicates the process of conversion, of changing one's way of life. That is to say, it has the same significance for Francis as it has in the Gospel and refers to the *metanoia*, the change of heart, which Christ and John the Baptist preached. The other ten examples concern the sacrament of penance, confession. Now, "penance," in the sense of conversion, is found almost exclusively in the texts addressed to "Christian religious" (seven times in the two *Letters to the Faithful*) and in passages referring, not to the friars, but to people in general (eight times—RegNB 12:4; 21:3,7f.; 23:4,7; 1EpCust 6). Only three texts deal with the friars (Test 1—Francis himself: Test 26 and EpOrd 44—the other friars), and here again reference is to living the Gospel life. In the *First Letter to the Faithful*, a chapter heading reads "Those who do not do penance." Here Francis advises the friars, when they are preaching, to urge "all those . . . who are not living in penance" (1EpFid 2:1; 2EpFid 63) to "perform worthy fruits of penance" (RegNB 21:3). From this, we can gather that some Christians, cleric or lay, men or women, had made the decision to take the Good News seriously and to meet the demands of the Gospel as fully as possible. Such people were called "religious" and were invited to live according to "the command and counsels" of the Gospel (2EpFid 39), as did the Poor Men of Lyons and the Humiliati.

The *Second Letter to the Faithful* proposes a mode of Gospel life which, in itself, could apply to all Christians. It certainly includes people who remained living in general society. We know that they did not have to dispose of their possessions since they were encouraged to give alms (2EpFid 30f.) and could still make bad use of their property (vv.72-80). It is surprising to find that material poverty, the renunciation of property and the restricted use of things, is not recommended or even mentioned, although such poverty was so prominent in the lives of the friars.

Among those to whom the letter was addressed there were some, perhaps magistrates or priests, who had the power to judge others, a function which demanded discernment and especially mercy on their part (vv.28f.). In fact, certain counsels in this letter presuppose the existence of some type of community, a kind of "fraternity" of penitents (vv.40-44). In this regard, the letter speaks about the connection between authority and obedience. The person to whom the power of demanding obedience was confided was to consider himself "the lesser" (*minor*) and the servant of the others. He was to exhort and support them patiently and humbly, never getting angry with those who were at fault. The others agreed to place themselves under "the yoke of service and holy obedience," to the extent they had undertaken and within certain limits. This passage in the letter uses the word "brothers" three times, which, along with the theme of obedience, would seem to imply at least an embryonic form of community.

Therefore, the two *Letters to the Faithful* were addressed to a group of fervent Christians who had not "left the world" but were living in everyday society. Yet there is no mention of family life, relationships between men and women, marriage and social connections. But Francis's preoccupations were not what we would be concerned about. Perhaps he thought it enough to give everyone an outline of a way of life as the Gospels do, leaving to each one the choice and the freedom to apply the Gospel teachings in their own lives.

Nevertheless, two of Francis's texts, the *Letter to the Clergy* and the *Letter to the Rulers of the Peoples*, show that he was not always content with providing general recommendations but wished to challenge some sectors of society about the way they performed their own particular duties. Thus, to a greater or lesser degree, clerics were responsible for abuses connected with the Eucharist. Therefore, Francis sternly called upon such neglectful clerics to "amend [their] ways" quickly and to observe scrupulously "the precepts of the Lord and the constitutions of holy Mother Church." Otherwise, they would "be bound to give an account before our Lord Jesus Christ on the day of judgement" (EpCler 10-14). He also made a specific request to the "mayors and consuls, magistrates and rulers," that is, the authorities in the more or less free cities of the time, to whose care the people had been confided (EpRect 7). He asked these officials to see to it that a "town crier" made a public announcement every evening "that praise and thanks [might] be given by all people to the all-powerful Lord God." While this letter was quite courteous in tone, it was still emphatic.

Francis knew about "the care and preoccupations" which the city authorities had and which could cause them to forget the Lord and His commandments. So, in no uncertain terms, he reminded them twice that the day of death was approaching inexorably for each one of them (vv.2,4: *sic transit gloria mundi . . .*). Then, gently but firmly, he advised them to "receive with joy the most holy Body and the most holy Blood of our Lord Jesus Christ in holy remembrance of Him" (v.6).

While Francis normally confined himself to stressing the basic duties demanded of all believers, he did, on occasion, remind his readers of other, more specific, obligations.

The Life of the Friars Minor

When the Lord revealed to Francis the way of life "according to the form of the Holy Gospel," he and the brothers whom the Lord had given him (Test 14), and the thousands who followed, adopted it in faith, put it into practice, and tested it in real life situations. This large group soon came to be called "Friars Minor," and Francis described and legislated for their way of life in texts which make up about a third of his writings. These texts are the *Rules* (RegNB, RegB, RegErm), the testaments (Test, TestSen), and four letters (1EpCust, 2EpCust, EpOrd, EpMin). In the preceding pages, we have examined at length their general contents. But now we propose to consider and summarize only those things in them which seem to apply solely to the life of the friars.

"This the life of the Gospel of Jesus Christ"
(RegNB Prol.1)

Haec est vita evangelii Jesu Christi. This terse sentence can be interpreted in several ways—as "the life according to the Gospel," "the life which makes the Gospel come to life again," or "which makes Jesus Christ live again" (D. Dozzi). Francis used it as the title of the first and longer version of his *Rule* (RegNB). The word "Gospel" (used twenty-four times) is found mainly in those writings relating to the friars (nineteen times), in the *Second Letter to the Faithful* (four times) and once in Admonition 3:1. It indicates, first, the book of the Gospels (sixteen times) and precedes quotations in formulas such as "the Lord says [or commands] in the Gospel" (eleven times), "according to the Gospel" (four times), "the word of the Gospel" (once).

Eight other examples refer, not to the text or the book of the Gospels, but to the message they contain, as in the formulas "to observe [or promise] the holy Gospel" (RegNB 5:17; 22:41; RegB 1:1; 12:14), "the perfection of the holy Gospel" (FormViv 1; BenBer 2; Test 14), and "the life of the Gospel of Jesus Christ" (RegNB Prol.1). These texts are found either in the *Rules* (five times) or in passages concerning the life of the friars. Thus, Francis only used the word "Gospel" in the comprehensive sense of "the Gospel message" to signify and define the plan of life he proposed to his friars and the Poor Ladies (FormViv 1). "The Most High Himself [had] revealed to [him] that [he] should live according to the form of the Holy Gospel" (Test 14). As we have seen, he described his *Earlier Rule* by saying: "This is the life of the Gospel of Jesus Christ." The *Later Rule* declares: "The rule and life of the Friars Minor is this: to observe the holy Gospel of our Lord Jesus Christ" (RegB 1:1; 12:14). Clare and Bernard chose to live according to "the perfection of the Holy Gospel" (FormViv; BenBer 2). We should note that, unlike the other movements of renewal in the Middle Ages, Francis never used the popular contemporary title, *vita apostolica* or *vita apostolorum*.

But what meaning did Francis give to the word, "Gospel," which he loved so much? It is usually said that he used it only to indicate texts relating to poverty, itinerant preaching, and living the apostolic life in poverty, which would be a definition of the life of the Friars Minor. But was this the case? The eight examples we have just mentioned do not provide an immediate answer to our question because, in fact, they refer in general to "a form of life," a coherent system, comprised of many elements, not all of which have the same "Gospel" importance. When, before quoting a text, Francis mentions the Gospel explicitly, what elements, what demands is he referring to? We shall be able to give a more precise and objective answer if we examine the texts in which he follows this practice.

Of sixteen mentions of this kind, four speak about the evil in the human heart (1EpFid 2:12; 2EpFid 37,69; RegNB 22:6), two refer to permissions (eating and drinking—RegNB 2:14; RegB 2:5), two urge perseverance (RegNB 2:10; RegB 2:13), two are about poverty (RegNB 2:14; RegB 2:5), and the other six concern, respectively, the promise of being acknowledged by the Father (RegNB 16:8), the commandment to love (2EpFid 18), the call to self-renunciation (Adm 3:1), to serve rather than to rule (RegNB 5:10), to avoid avarice and worldly cares (RegNB 10:11f.), and to receive the seed of the word of God in good soil (RegNB 22:16).

From these references, we can see that the Gospel life is not limited to external actions such as "sell[ing] everything" (RegNB 1:2), or "carry[ing] nothing for the journey" (RegNB 14:1). Instead, it means receiving the message of the Gospel as a whole, with all its revelations, promises, and various demands, without excluding or preferring any particular element. Thus, chapter 1 of the *Earlier Rule* quotes four Gospel texts whose main theme is "following Christ," "coming to Him," by selling one's possessions, renouncing self and family ties. These three requirements for following Christ are rewarded by the promise of a hundredfold return here and eternal life hereafter. Therefore, the Gospel is at once a demand and a promise.

In another important text, a kind of summary of what he had most at heart, Francis makes clear what the Gospel meant for him and what the friars should "hold on to," namely, "the words, the life and the teachings . . . of Him who humbled Himself to ask His Father for us and to make His name known to us" (RegNB 22:41). In the fullest sense, the Gospel was, for Francis, Christ Himself, revealing to us the Father's "name," that is, His nature as God, by His own life and words on earth and introducing us, by prayer, to knowledge of the Father.

The Central Theme of the Friars' Life

In particular, the *Earlier* and *Later Rules*, the *Rule for Hermitages* and the *Testament* describe the friars' life, which is composed of different elements—breaking with the world, prayer, common life, work, owning no property, begging, itinerancy, preaching as the occasion arises, a certain amount of structured regulation, and relationships with the Church. But do all these elements have the same value, or is there a hierarchy of values among them, with one central theme that supports and shapes the rest? And if there is a central theme, what is it?

In a remarkable essay based on his study of the *Testament*, G. Miccoli holds that this central theme is radical poverty, both spiritual as well as material. The summary of the friars' life which Francis gives in his *Testament* (vv.16-23) lends credence to this view—selling one's possessions, poverty in dress, prayer in churches, submission to everyone, manual labor, begging, and an ardent desire for peace. However, in his summary of the constituent elements of "the form of the Holy Gospel" revealed to him, Francis does not try to include everything or to indicate the main foundation of the Franciscan life. The *Testament of Siena* names only three points—fraternal charity, poverty, and fidelity to the Church. The *Testament* itself covers a wider range. It mentions Francis's conversion to the Gospel life as a result of his serving the lepers, the spiritual "sweetness" which accompanied this service (Test 1-3), and his faith in churches and priests in connection with the Eucharist. That is to say, the material details of the Gospel life as Francis understood that life have meaning and cohesion only when they are inspired by a theological vision.

The *Testament* simply recalls and summarizes the circumstances of the end of Francis's life and the early development of the Fraternity. If we are to have a proper understanding of this summary, we must read it in the light of the previously composed basic texts, the *Earlier* and *Later Rules*. Now, while these *Rules* repeat the description of the Franciscan life in almost the same order as the *Testament*, they emphasize strongly what seems to be the heart of the Gospel life, that is, the relationship of the soul with God. The *Earlier Rule* does this in the closing chapter of the first section (chap.17:5-19), urging the friars to die to self, to acquire true spiritual wisdom, and to attribute everything to God. This *Rule* ends with two additions, chapters 22 and 23, which we have already discussed several times and which describe the perfection of the friars' life and that of all believers.

Some may not consider these two passages to be central to Francis's Gospel plan or may regard them as being merely "spiritual" or "theological"—indeed, almost sheerly theoretical —in nature. But to make either of these assumptions would be to distort Francis's proposed way of life and reduce it to a program for external action only, which is easier to see and describe than the interior, spiritual life of the soul.

More condensed and, to a certain degree, less rich in detail than the *Earlier Rule*, the *Later Rule* does not neglect the central theme but repeats it when dealing with the occupations and commitments of the friars and with their work and studies. This *Later Rule* forcefully asserts that everything must be put at the service of "the Spirit of holy prayer and devotion" (RegB 5:2) and that the friars "must desire above all things to have the Spirit of the Lord and His holy manner of working, to pray always to Him with a pure heart" (RegB 10:8f.).

From these texts and from Francis's whole vision, which we have presented in this study, it is clear that the central theme of the friars' way of life consists in surrendering self in faith to God, who gave Himself totally to us (EpOrd 29). In this way, we learn to love and serve God and our neighbor (ExpPat 5) because "now that we have left the world, we have nothing else to do except follow the will of the Lord and to please Him" (RegNB 22:9).

Special Elements

Towards the end of his life, Francis wrote *Rules* for his followers, who by then numbered in the thousands. These *Rules* provided a rudimentary structure for the Fraternity and legislated for the mode of life of those who had been drawn to join him by their desire to live the Gospel life. His norms for that life contained six basic elements: prayer in common, community life, material poverty, daily work, being with the people, and maintaining close ties with the Church, all with a specifically missionary purpose.

Prayer in Common

This seems to have been the first element in the life of the friars, both in the *Rules* and in the *Testament* (v.18). For those who knew how to read, prayer was the Divine Office, the liturgical prayer of the Church, while, for the others, it consisted in the repetition of the Creed, the Our Father and the Glory be . . . , as prescribed in the *Rules*. Francis's directions regulating the friars' prayer were exclusively liturgical, and only in the *Letter to the Entire Order* did he touch on the spirit in which the Office was to be celebrated: ". . . with devotion before God . . . so that the voice may blend with the mind, and the mind be in harmony with God, in such a way that they may please God through purity of mind." To this fervent exhortation, Francis added a warning about "concentrating on the melody of the voice" and the desire to "charm the ears of the people with sweetness of voice" (EpOrd 40-42). We can see here, almost word for word, the Cistercian condemnation of the supposed liturgical excesses of Cluny.

But this dry outline does not do justice to the vision which Francis had of the importance of liturgical prayer as the first structured activity of his Fraternity. His *Rule for Hermitages* organized the whole life of the friar-hermits around the canonical hours. His two fervent invitatories to the Divine Office (LaudHor; ExhLd), his *Office of the Passion*, and the extent to which his writings are suffused with the liturgy are indicative of the theological and spiritual role which the celebration of the liturgy must have played in the life of the early Fraternity.

On the other hand, the official, communal prayer of the Divine Office presupposes solitary, individual interior prayer, which is a requirement for any kind of fervent Christian life. We have already considered this. Francis wished his friars to engage in continual prayer (RegNB 22:29; RegB 10:9) and not only his friars but every Christian, too (RegNB 23:11a; 2EpFid 21).

At the time when Francis was dictating his *Letter to the Entire Order*, perhaps around 1225, there were both "clerical and lay" brothers in his Fraternity (RegNB 3:3; 15:1; 17:5; 20:1; RegB 3:1-3; Test 38), of whom a relatively significant number were those "who are or who will be or who wish to be priests of the Most High" (EpOrd 14). There was no discrimination between clerical and lay brothers when it was a question of filling posts of responsibility, since both clerical and lay brothers could be ministers (RegB 7:2). However, the confessors for the brothers had to be "priests of our Order" (RegNB 20:1; RegB 7:2; EpMin 18) at a time when frequent confession was the common practice.

This letter was concerned principally with the celebration of the Mass, which was already a daily practice and which formed part of the liturgy of each day. Francis strongly emphasized the dignity of the friar-priests. They had the power to offer "the true Sacrifice of the most holy Body and Blood of our Lord Jesus Christ" and intimate contact with Christ, "who is now not about to die, but who is eternally victorious and glorified" (EpOrd 14;22f.). He urged these priests to celebrate Mass "purely . . . , with reverence and with a holy and pure intention, not for any mundane reason or out of fear or out of love for some person" (EpOrd 14). And he especially wished that they should not break the bonds of fraternity at the central moment of the day by private, individual celebration of the Mass. Therefore, he directed that

> only one Mass . . . [is] to be celebrated each day in the places in which the brothers stay. If, however, there should be more than one priest in that place, let one be content, for the sake of charity, to assist at the celebration of the other priest (EpOrd 30f.).

This request, which broke with the current practice of celebrating private Masses, can be explained only by Francis's very lively sense of community in relation to the Mass. So, while the dimension of the Eucharist as the ecclesial body of Christ does not appear in his writings, he shows it here by the way he emphasizes the community.

Community or Fraternity

Francis never called himself simply "Francis" but always "Brother Francis." He used the title "brother" more than any other (306 times), except that of "Lord" (410 times). He was the first legislator to call his religious group a "Fraternity" (nine times), as if the more usual terms "Order" or *religio* ("religious institution") did not succeed in saying what he believed should be the essence of a community based on the Gospel.

This Fraternity had certain minimal structures, such as chapters (RegNB 18; RegB 8), with vague juridical requirements; but local superiors were not mentioned. Provincial superiors were selected, by whom we do not know, to

> assign their brothers to the provinces and to the places where they are to be, and they should visit them

frequently and spiritually admonish and encourage them
(RegNB 4:2).

Since Francis excluded the titles of "Father" (*Abbas*—RegNB
22:34) and "Prior" (RegNB 6:3), these superiors were to be given the
name "minister," which was then spreading in the reform
movements, such as the Carthusians, the Humiliati, and the
Trinitarians. That is, the superiors were to be servants of the
community, as is made clear by the double title which is so often
associated with Francis, *minister et servus*.

These "servants" were not to become attached to their offices
(RegNB 17:4; Adm 4) or be domineering or act like masters (RegNB
4:6; 5:9-12). On the contrary, they were to show their brothers such
kindness and "be so approachable that these brothers can speak
and deal with the ministers as masters with their servants" (RegB
10:5f.). This return to a Gospel concept of authority as humble
service and "the washing of feet" (RegNB 6:4; Adm 4) was as
revolutionary as Francis's choice of radical poverty, if not even
more so, a point that has not been sufficiently stressed. One of the
brothers was to be "the minister general and servant of the entire
fraternity" (RegB 8:1;9:2), as Francis was until the end of his life.

These ministers had the same power as Francis himself, a
power which he exercised very firmly, as we see from the formulas
he often used: "I strictly command . . ." (six times), "under
obedience" (three times), or "I wish . . ." (nine times in the
Testament). Nevertheless, especially in the *Earlier Rule*, we can
sense that he was wary of the exercise of authority and feared that
it might lead to an abuse of power and become domineering. For
that reason, he reminded the ministers of all the Gospel warnings
about the use of authority (Mt 20:25f.,28; Lk 22:26). Moreover, he
directed that "all the brothers who are subject to the ministers and
servants should reasonably and diligently consider the actions of
these ministers and servants" (RegNB 5:3) and take steps to correct
them when necessary (RegNB 5:3-6), as they were also to do for
each other.

Francis wished that all his "blessed brothers should diligently
obey [their ministers] in those matters which concern the well-
being of their souls and which are not contrary to our life" (RegNB

4:3). Apparently, he was anxious to ensure this limitation of the friars' duty to obey, for he comes back to it several times (RegNB 5:2; RegB 10:1-3; Adm 3:7). But, in thus safeguarding the friars' spiritual liberty, he left the door open for subjective inter-pretations of the *Rule*. For the rest, we can see in him an evolution towards greater strictness as regards obedience and its limits. As time passed, he lost some of his confidence in the brothers' spiritual judgment and in the freedom allowed them "to obey their ministers in all those things which they have promised the Lord to observe and which are not against their consciences and our Rule" (RegB 10:3). Admonition 3 and the *Testament* show a certain hard-ening of his attitude in response to real life situations.

Yet his overall concept of obedience was a balanced one. For example, his description of obedience in chapter 5 of the *Earlier Rule* (vv.13-17) is remarkable. There, he indicates three areas of obedience. The first is that in which the friars persevere "in the commands of the Lord, which they have promised through the holy Gospel and their life" (RegNB 5:17). In other words, the primary, basic obedience demanded of the friars is to live according to the promises and demands of the Gospel. The second area of obedience is meant to ensure that

> . . . [no] brother should do evil or say something evil to another; . . . on the contrary, through the charity of the Spirit, they should voluntarily serve and obey one another. And this is the true and holy obedience of our Lord Jesus Christ (RegNB 5:13-15).

This is the obedience in which Christ lived, which He proposes to us, and which He makes possible.

The third type of obedience to the ministers (RegNB 4:3; RegB 10:2f.) finds its true place within these two overlapping areas. It is an exercise in freedom: doing or saying what is "good" and "not contrary to the superior's will . . . is true obedience" (Adm 3:4). It is "giv[ing] up [one's] own will for God" (RegB 10:2): and it is "perfect obedience" when the subject, in spite of not agreeing with a superior's command, does not "abandon him" (Adm 3:7-10).

We have already spoken at length about the relationships of the friars with each other and about the need for charity between them. Francis believed that brotherly, even motherly, love should prevail in the community as the first of the three qualities which he wished to see among the friars—love for one another, love of poverty and fidelity to the Church—as he said in his *Testament Written in Siena*: "As a sign that they remember my blessing and my testament, let them always love one another" (TestSen 3).

Material Poverty

Although the plan of Christian life which Francis proposed to all believers was radical and mystical, it did not demand material poverty. He merely exhorted the faithful to give alms (2EpFid 30) and to avoid using their possessions to defraud or deceive others (cf. 2EpFid 72-80). But he did make poverty an integral part of the life of the friars and the Poor Ladies. Because of his clear and uncompromising insistence of poverty, it quickly came to be regarded as the main element of the Franciscan way of life. This was despite the fact that the prescriptions of the two *Rules* and the *Testament* were far from being as literal and as rigid as they seemed and even though other, less material, demands were just as radical.

The first thing candidates to the Fraternity were required to do was to follow the Gospel instruction to sell whatever they owned and give the money to the poor (Mt 19:21; RegNB 2:4,11; RegB 2:5f.; Test 16). However, the aspirant was to do this only "if he wishes and is able to do so spiritually and without any impediment," but, if not, "let him leave these things behind; and this suffices for him" (RegNB 2:4,11). The friars were to wear clothes that were "poor" (RegNB 2:14; RegB 2:16; Test 16) and confined to essentials. Following the Gospel directive (Mt 6:9), they were allowed only "one tunic" (Test 16) but could have two, if necessary or desirable (RegNB 2:8,13; RegB 2:9,14); and they were permitted to wear shoes when the need arose (RegB 2:15).

The definitive *Later Rule* formally forbade the use of money and even all contact with it. Yet this same *Rule*, while rejecting money so vehemently, still allowed it to be handled when it was required to help the sick friars or the lepers (RegNB 7:3,7,10). But the truly radical way in which the Franciscans, both friars and Poor Ladies, broke with the contemporary forms of religious life was in their renunciation of all property and hence of every assured means of subsistence. This *Later Rule* stated quite categorically that: "The brothers shall acquire nothing as their own, neither a house nor a place nor anything at all" (RegB 6:1; cf. RegNB 7:13; Test 17). Because the friars had no other source of revenue, they had to earn the necessities of life by working for others (RegNB 7:1-10; RegB 5; Test 20f.). And when that failed, as most likely it usually did, they had to "seek alms from door to door," despite any repugnance or shame they might feel in doing so (Test 22; RegNB 9:1-9; RegB 6:2f.). This collective poverty introduced something quite new in religious life, apart, perhaps, from the beginnings of the Order of Gramont. Moreover, due to socio-economic factors, it created new problems which, in the course of the centuries, the Order has tried to solve in one way or another by endeavouring to combine utopian ideals with harsh realities. In his last document, the *Testament*, Francis himself gave an example when he allowed the friars to accept "churches or other poor dwellings or anything that is built for them." He allowed this only if these things were "in harmony with that holy poverty" which they had promised and provided that the friars should "always be guests there as pilgrims and strangers" (OffPass Ps.38:13; 1Pet 2:11).

The Franciscans treasured this socio-economic poverty as their very own distinctive mark. That is why Francis exclaimed:

> This is that summit of highest poverty which has established you, my most beloved brothers, as heirs and kings of the kingdom of heaven; it has made you poor in the things of this world but exalted you in virtue. Let this be your portion which leads into the land of the living. Dedicating yourselves totally to this, my most beloved brothers, do not wish to have anything else forever under heaven for the sake of our Lord Jesus Christ (RegB 6:4-6).

But these eloquent words were not in praise of mere material poverty, which, properly understood and taken in its spiritual context, is simply part of that supreme poverty about which we have spoken before. As Francis taught in his commentary on the beatitude of the poor in spirit (Adm 14), true poverty does not consist simply in external actions, such as prayer or mortifications, etc., but in hating ourselves, loving those who strike us on the

cheek, and not being angry when we are hurt or deprived of what
we think is our due.

Francis considered material poverty to be an essential
component of the friars' vocation, but he did not ask it of other
Christians to whom he had proposed all the other Gospel demands
(2EpFid). Therefore, he believed that a full Gospel life was
possible without practising this form of poverty.

Daily Life

The *Rule for Hermitages* prescribed an organized daily routine but
only for the special way of life reserved for those friars "who wish
to live religiously in hermitages." The canonical hours of the
daytime and nighttime Divine Office formed the main framework
of this routine, with time allowed for meals and contacts with
those friars who took care of the material needs of the hermit's
life. In the ordinary communities also, the friars came together to
celebrate the Divine Office (EpOrd 41f.) and, whenever possible,
the Mass as well. At other times, the friars were engaged in doing
manual work or in minor forms of administration for others, by
which they earned the necessities of life, but always while acting
with discernment. Others went begging for food, not only for
themselves, but also for the other friars, whom they were urged to
"love and care for . . . in all those things in which God will give
[them] grace" (RegNB 9:10f.). The sequence of chapters in the
Earlier Rule describes the daily life of the friars: prayer (chap. 1),
life together (4-6), work and money (7,8), and begging (9). The order
of daily life is somewhat different in the *Later Rule*: prayer
(chap.3), money (4), work (5) and begging (6), while the *Testament*
(vv.18-22) divides the friars' tasks into prayer, work, and begging.
Both *Rules* stress the duty of caring and providing for the sick
friars (RegNB 10; RegB 6), which must have presented problems for
a group that was not yet fully settled.

"Going about the world"

The monastic Orders in general took vows of stability and totally
rejected the idea that monks could be *vagi*, "vagrants," wandering
about away from their abbeys. But, while Francis was not aware of

it, his way of life was similar to the monasticism of St. Martin of Tours, because he did not withdraw from the world.

Even though he and his friars preferred to live in solitary places (RegErm), their need to work for a living and their frequent moves brought them into contact with the world of ordinary people, to whom they "proclaimed . . . exhortation and praise" (RegNB 21:10), as the occasion arose.

The "world" was not simply the Christian world but also that of "the Saracens and other nonbelievers," among whom the brothers were permitted to go when inspired by God to do so. While the Crusaders fought against the Saracens with weapons, Francis wished his friars to "live spiritually among [them] . . . not to engage in arguments or disputes but to be subject to every human creature for God's sake and to acknowledge that they are Christians." The brothers were to preach the word of God there "when they [saw] that it please[d] the Lord" (RegNB 16:1-7).

"Going about the world" (RegNB 14:1; 15:1; RegB 3:1) implied that the friars were to go among people by simply moving around from place to place to work or serve others. They might bear witness to the Gospel by their presence or by preaching when the occasion offered. Preaching properly so called, that is, in the official canonical form, was permitted to those friars who had been examined and approved for that work (RegNB 17:1f.; RegB 9) but was not an essential part of the friars' life, as it was for the Dominicans, the Order of Preachers. The *Rules* mention preaching only as a kind of appendix to the Franciscan way of life and do not count it among the basic elements of that life, while the *Testament* (Test 25) refers to it simply in passing.

It was only with the historical development of the Order that preaching assumed the important place it had later in the activities of the friars. Yet, on the other hand, Francis told the brothers that "whenever it may please them, all my brothers can proclaim this or a like exhortation and praise among all the people with the blessing of God." And he then provided a sample "sermon" which combined theology and ethics, including praise of the creating Trinity, a change of life-style resulting in love of neighbor, and expectation of the life to come (RegNB 21).

Besides preaching in words, the friars "should preach by their deeds" (RegNB 17:3). The way the friars were to go among people was summed up in the *Later Rule* (RegB 3:10-14), which repeated the recommendations given in the *Earlier Rule* (RegNB 11; 14; 16:5; cf. Test 19,23):

> I counsel, admonish and exhort my brothers in the Lord Jesus Christ, that, when they go about the world, they do not quarrel or fight with words or judge others; rather, let them be meek, peaceful and unassuming, gentle and humble, speaking courteously to everyone, as is becoming. And they should not ride on horseback unless they are forced by manifest necessity or infirmity. In whatever house they enter, let them say: Peace to this house. And, according to the holy Gospel, they are free to eat of whatever food is set before them (RegB 3:10-14).

This exhortation is a good summary of what Francis meant by the title "Friar Minor"—one who has brotherly love for everyone, is affable to all, never imposes on others, serves everybody, brings peace, and waits to be accepted by those whom he wishes to serve. The friars' first mission among people, even more important than preaching, was to cultivate the attitudes Francis described. He was aware of the difficulties his brothers would encounter—the temptation to think they were better than others and to judge them (RegNB 17:5-7; RegB 2:17), to engage in arguments and disputes (RegNB 11:1-3), to seek protection and privileges (Test 25f.), to have suspicious or frankly immoral dealings with women (RegNB 12; 13; RegB 11). But instead of having his brothers cut themselves off completely from "the world," he preferred to describe the way they should "go about" that "world" (RegB 3:10).

Links with the Church

The prologue to the *Earlier Rule* and chapters 1 and 12 of the *Later Rule* bind Francis's Fraternity to the Church. In the name of all his brothers, Francis promised "obedience and reverence to the Lord Pope Honorius and his canonically elected successors," a promise of loyalty to the Church which was like that which a vassal made to his liege lord (RegNB Prol 3; RegB 1:2;12:4). Yet this was no mere legal formality but the expression of a deep faith. The last lines of the *Later Rule* affirm:

> ... so that, always submissive and prostrate at the feet of the same holy Church, and steadfast in the Catholic faith, we may observe the poverty and the humility and the holy Gospel of our Lord Jesus Christ which we have firmly promised (RegB 12:4).

In his writings, Francis spoke of the Church as centered on, and unified by, Rome. He knew the Church's Roman representatives personally—Innocent III, Honorius III, and Cardinal Hugolino, who later became Gregory IX; and he mentions the Church's personnel—clerics, religious (RegNB 19:3), and theologians (Test 6-9; TestSen 5)—whom he wished to be regarded as "lords" and shown every mark of respect (RegNB 19:3). Such a bond of union with the Church guaranteed the authenticity of the friars' Catholic faith. As we have already seen, the brothers were firmly rooted in this wide-horizoned faith and found in it the strength to live up to the poverty and humility of the Gospel.

Francis was very solicitous for the orthodoxy of his brothers' faith and demanded that: "All the brothers must be Catholics and live and speak in a Catholic manner. But if any of them has strayed from the Catholic faith and life, in word or deed . . . , he should be completely expelled from our fraternity (RegNB 19:2; Test 31)," while candidates for the Order were to be "diligently examined . . . concerning the Catholic faith" (RegB 2:2).

The Fraternity's links with the Church, and especially their having direct recourse to the Holy See, can be partially explained by their geographic nearness to Rome and by the growing contemporary emphasis on Rome as the center of the Church's authority. In addition, the Roman Curia was undoubtedly exerting pressure in this direction. Yet Francis himself must have grasped intuitively the pre-eminent place which the Church in Rome occupied as the center of Catholic unity and universality, and that is why he had such faith in it. Many modern biographers of Francis hold that there were conflicts and tensions between him and Rome. But, whether or not this was the case, there is no trace of such conflict or tension in his writings. Instead, the astonishing thing is that the Church officially approved and confirmed documents as innovative and as lacking in legal structures as Francis's two *Rules*.

The Mission of the Friars

> Listen, sons of the Lord and my brothers, pay attention to my words (Acts 2:14). Incline the ear (Is 55:3) of your heart, and obey the voice of the Son of God. Observe His commands with your whole heart, and fulfil His counsels with a perfect mind. Give praise to Him since He is good (Ps 135:1), and exalt Him by your deeds (Tob 13:6), for He has sent you into the entire world for this reason (cf.Tob 13:4), that in word and deed you may give witness to His voice and bring everyone to know that there is no one who is all-powerful except Him (Tob 13:4). Persevere in discipline and holy obedience and with a firm purpose fulfil what you have promised to Him. The Lord God offers Himself to us as to His children (Heb 12:7) [EpOrd 5-11].

Today, when we wish to define the mission of a group in society or in the Church, we try to describe what the group does, its main activities. However, the texts which govern the life of the Friars Minor are nothing like that: they do not describe the friars' activities or the services they render but only their way of life.

This is especially evident in the solemn text, composed of biblical references and quoted above, with which the *Letter to the Entire Order* opens and which is the founding charter of the friars' special mission. The brothers have been "sent into the entire world" to "give witness to [the] voice," that is, the words, "of the Son of God." This message was inspired by the Canticle of Tobit, as used in the Divine Office. Although the Canticle is short, it is full of meaning, teaching everyone to know that "there is no one who is all-powerful except [God]." This is reminiscent of the Moslem declaration that "God is great," which Francis must have heard proclaimed from the minarets of Damietta in Egypt.

But this Omnipotence is not solely and primarily a Creative Power but is also Kindness and Love: "Give praise to Him since He is good and exalt Him by your deeds." Nor are these deeds external achievements but consist in an attitude of welcome that seems passive, an attitude of listening, as we see from the four words, "listen," "incline the ear," "obey" (from *ob-audire*), and the "ear," in the phrase "the ear of your heart." Such a listening heart receives the Gospel message—the revelation of God, His love and His demands—and keeps it fully, obeying the commandments and the counsels, by "persever[ing] in discipline and holy obedience and with a firm and good purpose." Yet this message does not impose a heavy yoke upon us because it is not an admonitory sermon but a meeting with "the Lord God [who] offers Himself to us as to His children."

According to this biblical "program," the friars' mission consists in proclaiming the mystery of God, of His all-powerful love and the effects which these realities have on those who accept them, namely, hearing and welcoming the Word, following the Gospel way and persevering to the end. The friars proclaim these things mainly through their lives, but also through their words, which explain their message and their way of life. This is their *kerygma*. The heart of their mission, of their message, is there—and everything else, their way of life and its structures which the *Rules* prescribe, are at the service of that message.

The Poor Ladies

Until very recently, no texts relating to Clare and her sisters were listed among those writings which were fully accepted as Francis's. It was not until 1978 that a poem by Francis in the Umbrian dialect, entitled *Canticle of Exhortation to St. Clare and Her Sisters*, was discovered and published. This poem was composed around the same time as the *Canticle of Brother Sun* and was dedicated to the "Poor Sisters" at San Damiano. In the writings which Clare herself left us, her *Rule*, *Testament*, four *Letters to Agnes of Prague*, and a *Blessing*, she quotes only from two short documents from Francis— the *Form of Life*, which she received at the beginning of her religious life, and the *Last Will*, written for her, which dates from the end of Francis's life. But she does mention "many writings" of his, none of which have come down to us. Clare generously attributes to Francis himself the composition of her *Rule*. This, however, was not strictly the case since, on her own initiative, she had adopted the *Rule* which Francis had written for his brothers and modified and added to it as needed for her sisters.

Of the two texts composed by Francis which Clare incorporated into chapter 6 of her *Rule*, the first, the *Form of LIfe*, contains Francis's promise to the sisters, and the other, the *Last Will*, refers to fidelity to poverty. In the *Form of Life*, Francis assured the sisters:

> Because by divine inspiration you have made yourselves daughters and servants of the Most High King, the heavenly Father, and have espoused yourselves to the Holy Spirit, choosing to live according to the perfection of the holy Gospel, I resolve and promise for myself and for my brothers always to have that same loving care and special solicitude for you as I have for [my brothers].

His concept of the Poor Ladies' vocation was a decidedly Trinitarian one. Considering that he composed this text as early as the beginning of Clare's religious life, about 1214-1215, it is surprising to see the maturity and depth which his theological and spiritual insight had reached so soon after his conversion.

The sisters' choice of the Gospel life was more than an ascetical gesture of breaking away from the current social structures. Theirs was a life of radical poverty lived out in the context of the full Gospel demands. This choice of theirs was not merely an ordinary exercise of human free will but was a grace, an inspiration from God. In obeying the Gospel of Christ and its demands, they came closer to the Father, becoming daughters of the Most High King of heaven as well as His servants, and the Spirit accomplished in them the mysterious nuptials that are His specific work.

As we have seen, Francis uses these same words of the Virgin Mary in the Antiphon in his *Office of the Passion*. If we were able to determine which of these two texts, the *Form of Life* or the Antiphon, was the older, we would know to whom he first applied these words, to Mary or to the sisters.

The Roman Curia brought pressure to bear on Clare to renounce "the privilege of poverty," the privilege of not owning anything. But Francis, who was nearing the end of his life, sent her and her sisters a final message in his *Last Will*, affirming his own determination to live always in poverty and courteously addressing them as "my ladies":

I, little brother Francis, wish to follow the life and poverty of our most high Lord Jesus Christ and of His holy mother and to persevere in this until the end; and I ask and counsel you, my ladies, to live always in this most holy life and poverty. And keep most careful watch that you never depart from this by reason of the teaching or advice of anyone.

The most striking feature of these two texts, which Clare carefully preserved and incorporated into her *Rule*, is their theological dimension. In both of them, but especially in the first one, Francis stresses the mystical elements of poverty. He did so because it is through the narrow gate of poverty that we follow Christ and His mother to take part in a family marriage feast which the Father celebrates with His children, the nuptials of the Spirit.

While the passages which Clare quotes refer to specific events—such as the choice of a radical form of life, Francis's concern for the sisters, and misunderstandings and pressures from outside—they also emphasize the spiritual side of the Poor Ladies' life.

The *Canticle of Exhortation to St. Clare and Her Sisters* is a poetic rhymed piece, composed to be sung, with striking and imaginative descriptions. The sisters, "the little poor ones," had heard the Lord's call and had "come together from many parts and provinces" of Italy. Some of them were "weighed down by sickness," and others were fatigued by caring for the invalids. They lived mainly on alms, but because it was not always easy to achieve a proper balance in using the alms received, Francis besought them to use alms "with discernment." He exhorted them to "live always in truth" and to "die in obedience." To those who might be tempted to pine after "the life without," that is, life in the world outside the monastery, he pointed out that the life of the Spirit is better. He reminded those who were ill and those who were wearing themselves out in nursing them of the rewards promised to those who suffer trials in peace. They will receive "a very high price" for their suffering: "Each one of you will be crowned queen in heaven with the Virgin Mary."

For a more detailed description of the Poor Ladies' life, we must have recourse to Clare's own writings. Although she passed on to us only two fragments composed by Francis, she had received other documents from him. Moreover, in developing her own original spirituality and organizing her sisters' way of life, she had followed the advice and counsel of Francis, her spiritual father and friend.

To conclude this chapter on particular vocations, we should note certain points. Most of Francis's practical directions appear in those texts which he addressed to the three groups mentioned above, the "penitents," the Friars Minor, and the sisters at San Damiano. First, he sets down the basic facts of the Christian life—the knowledge and love of God and His salvation; the Gospel and our need to follow it. In the *Second Letter to the Faithful*, and particularly in the *Rules* and the other texts relating to the friars, we find prescriptions for living the Gospel in real life situations. Francis describes the Gospel of poverty and humility in terms of the age in which he lived. He provides the structures that were needed for community life at that time—ministers, chapters, obedience, and authority. His attitude to material possessions was a complete break with the socio-economic order of the era, which was also that of the Church. He counsels rejection of possessions and money, wearing poor clothing, serving or doing manual work for others in order to earn a living, and having recourse to alms and thereby identifying with the poorest members of society (RegNB 9:2).

The group's inner conviction of the need for total renunciation of self and everything else showed itself spectacularly in their life-style. While it is true that Francis sometimes quotes Gospel texts to justify his mode of life (for example, in RegB 2:5), it would be wrong to accuse him of interpreting the Scriptures literally. Most of the time, even his literal application of texts has subtle shades of meaning and makes allowances for special circumstances, as we can see from the conclusion of the chapter on begging, undoubtedly the most unusual and radical demand of all: "In times of manifest necessity, all the brothers should take care of their needs, as the Lord gives them the grace, since "necessity knows no law"" (RegNB 9:16).

When a radical ideal is not expressed outwardly, it remains invisible, and its very existence can be doubted. But when such an ideal is put into practice, it becomes bound up with definite people, situations, and historical epochs. It is no longer abstract and absolute but only concrete and relative. Finding a balance between the ideal and the real, the absolute and the relative, that is, fulfilling the requirements of reality without losing sight of the ideal, is a difficult task and one that is never fully accomplished. The history of the Franciscan Order is proof of that.

Part III

Interpretation and Relevance
of
Francis's Vision

Chapter 7

Interpretation and Relevance
of
Francis's Vision

Throughout this study, we have tried to be as objective as possible in interpreting Francis's message as it appears in his writings. But what criterion can we use to judge whether or not we have been successful? Francis's vision was profoundly influenced by the faith which he had been taught at home, at school, and in church and which was deepened and brought to maturity by his secular and religious experiences. From his faith, he had learned his special way of looking at God, humanity, the world, and its history. It is by this faith that we must judge his vision. This will not be an easy task because no one can claim to understand and express perfectly the totality and balance of a faith which cannot be confined within the strict limits of any one system of theology. Hence, as we attempt our task, we are fully aware of its difficulties.

Francis's Originality

Using as our base the outlines which Francis himself set down in two key texts (RegNB 23; 2EpFid), we have presented his views on God and humanity, that is, his theology and his anthropology. Is there anything original in these admittedly far-ranging views? But how can a theology be original? It cannot be a matter of introducing new elements or proposing a radically different hierarchy of the old ones. This is so because, even when biblical revelation is systematized and interpreted by a particular theology, it is still a body of knowledge to which nothing can be added and from which nothing can be taken away. It has its own internal cohesion in which the truths of faith are interlinked in a balanced hierarchy, truths such as the Triune God, the mission of the Son and the Spirit in the world, and our place in the plan of salvation. Every theology and every spirituality that claims to be Christian must respect these facts, accept them wholeheartedly, and hand them on faithfully.

Francis's writings were not original in the sense that they contained anything hitherto unknown or suggested a new way of looking at old truths. But they were original because, with their own dignity, they conveyed the totality and balance of the biblical vision. Moreover, they were original because they were written by a man without formal theological training, as he himself admitted: "I am ignorant and unlearned" (EpOrd 39; cf. Test 19; VPLaet 11). But despite his lack of schooling, his writings are amazingly wide-ranging yet precise, especially those which were occasioned by specific circumstances.

His Theology

When Francis writes about God, he does so primarily in reference to the Trinity, but not in an abstract way. He concentrates on the Father, from whom the Son proceeds, and who is the Source of every divine initiative and work, the Primary Object of praise and prayer—in short, the Beginning and the End of everything. In Francis's writings, the Spirit appears almost always as an unobtrusive Presence, dynamic, suffusing everything, and introducing a spiritual dimension into everything. It is clear that it was from St. John's Gospel that Francis derived this approach to the mystery of the Father.

Francis's christology, while insisting on the divinity of the Word, "the Most High, the Lord, the God of the universe," also emphasizes the humility and poverty which Christ showed in His Incarnation and in the Eucharist. As the Church does in the *Credo*, Francis regards Christ's mission as occurring in three stages—His Incarnation, His Passion and Resurrection, and His Second Coming. This view, too, is Johannine.

One particularly original point concerns the Eucharist, which, for Francis, is the center of Christ's living, glorious presence on earth, under the appearances of bread and wine. He links this sacramental presence in the celebration of Mass more to the word than to the community. In this vision, however, there are some omissions, for, although he stresses Christ's words, he does not emphasize His earthly life. Then, too, devotion to Christ's humanity is not given the same prominence in Francis's vision as it was normally afforded in the Middle Ages, or as it was with St. Clare, for example. Finally, the ecclesial dimension of the Eucharist as the Body of Christ does not appear there either.

Nevertheless, in Francis's writings, the Church is very closely linked to the Eucharist on another level, namely, by his reverence for the priesthood. In his eyes, the priest's principal, if not exclusive function, is the service of the sacrament of the Eucharist. Even so, for him, the Church is not made up of clerics alone but is the people of God, with their various functions and positions in society. Although the Church exists and works in this world, it is connected with and looks forwards to the world beyond. Mary, in her two-fold role as servant and glorious Lady, both prefigures and shows us now the destiny that inspires and awaits the Church on earth. Here again, we must remark on the absence of the Pauline theme of the Church as the Body of Christ.

His Vision of Humanity

We humans occupy a central place in Francis's vision, and he never refers to God without including us, God's human partners, as if it is impossible to encounter Him without meeting us.

The picture Francis paints of us in his writings is one of violent contrasts. When we read some of his descriptions, we are left with the impression that we are utterly corrupt and decadent, "having nothing of our own but our vices and sins." This would seem to be Pauline pessimism accentuated by Augustinian overtones.

But when we examine this image more closely, we find that our human greatness and dignity are also taken into account. This sovereign greatness, this "excellence," is based on "the holy love with which God loves" us whom He has made in His image and likeness. From this love come the innumerable gifts, qualities, and abilities which God has given us and which we should contemplate in wonder.

In God's original plan, we were to retain this greatness and dignity here and hereafter. But, "through our own fault," we were physically and morally brought to ruin. Francis leaves us in no doubt about our corruption, our perverted hearts that produce nothing but evil, and he is insistent that we recognize and acknowledge our true, miserable condition. He then goes on to propose a course of conduct, a spiritual program, which will take into account both the good and bad aspects of our humanity and help us to make the best of both. He sums up this program in two simple words, poverty and humility. We must recognize the two contradictory facets of our nature, the good that is in us, that *is* us, and the bottomless abyss of evil that yawns within us. So, as really poor people, we must return all good things to God, without claiming any of them as our own. We must attribute to ourselves only the evil which disfigures us and for which we are partly responsible.

Francis's poverty, then, consists, first, in acknowledging that everything good comes from God and returning it to Him in thanksgiving; and second, in recognizing that all we have of our own is our weakness and sin, so that we can present ourselves to the Divine Physician, who alone can restore us to health.

This state of poverty keeps us humble, for it shows us the truth about ourselves, our gifts, and our defects. As a result, we can go among people as their servants, submissive to everyone, not out of servility, but because we respect and accept others with a fraternal love. Because we are brothers to all, to everyone living and dead, we recognize a resemblance between themselves and us, a common origin and a family affection. The external poverty which Francis proposed to his brothers and sisters is only an outward sign of, and introduction to, this inner self-deprivation.

Francis's views on humanity were not limited to the individual and his or her perfection. He also dealt with interpersonal relationships, both community and occasional. However, the social dimension, in the family or in society, to which people are so sensitive nowadays, is absent from his writings, and he does not mention it even in his *Second Letter to the Faithful*, where we would have expected to find it.

Approach and Style

As we have noted, the basic structure of Francis's overall vision, which includes humanity as well as God, follows the pattern of the Church's *Credo*, but with some original additions. The mystery of the Father, Creator of all, is strongly emphasized and considered at length. As regards the Son, Francis's insistence on the Eucharist under its aspect of an active Presence is an interesting development. But the most unusual feature of Francis's message is the prominent place he gives to humans. We are tempted to say that the great proclamation of faith in chapter 23 of the *Earlier Rule* is devoted as much to us and to our destiny as to the Father's working in history through the Son and the Holy Spirit.

Francis's texts are *theological*, although they are not notable for their speculative approach or development of thought. In fact, his only venture into theological speculation was not particularly outstanding for its clarity (EpOrd 32f.), and, apart from chapter 23 of the *Earlier Rule*, he does not give a comprehensive overview of his work. Instead, he proceeds by stressing particular points and evoking key themes in salvation history—the Father's majesty and love, the Son's sacrifice for us, and the sanctifying action of the Holy Spirit—but in no sustained, systematic fashion. In addition, he appears to have found it difficult to write about God because he seems to have been torn between a desire to use God's name and reluctance to do so.

Although what he says about God and humanity obviously comes from intense personal experience, he never provides a subjective description of such experiences, with the possible exception of the "sweetness of soul and body" which he felt when serving the lepers (Test 3). He was a "mystic" in the sense that he had been sorely tried by God and his neighbor (Pseudo-Dionysius's *theía pathein*), but, unlike other mystics, he neither analyzed nor recorded his experiences. His counsels and exhortations, especially the *Admonitions*, are similar to the sayings of the Fathers of the Desert. When we compare his works with the usual writings of the mystics, we find that his moral teaching, unlike theirs, is always based on theology, as is the case especially with the introduction to his *Second Letter to the Faithful*.

His writings on God and humanity are never abstract and never set out to define and classify each subject. Instead, they are *narrative*, recalling the course of events, including the whole sweep of salvation history (RegNB 23), or, in more detail, the story of Christ's life and death (2EpFid 3-14). He favored confessional *proclamations*, in which he bore witness to what is essential and where every word had its own weight of meaning. He especially liked to express himself in prayer of praise but did not confine his praise of God to these prayers. Whenever he touched upon any important matter, his praise sprang up spontaneously and rose in an exultant song (e.g. RegNB 17:17-19; 2EpFid 61f.). His "theology" is lyrical in tone, and, in it, he uses a profusion of nouns and adjectives but without ever losing his natural simplicity of expression. While using ordinary, everyday words, and almost without verbal imagery, he could speak clearly and tellingly about the most profound truths.

If we read quickly through Francis's writings, we get the impression that he has nothing new to say to us since we have heard it all before in the Gospel. But if we take the time to absorb the full meaning of his words, then, under the apparent banality of his writing, we discover an unexpected wealth of truth.

Relevance of His Message

No matter how limited our knowledge of the Gospel and its message may be, we shall find that Francis's writings have a familiar ring because they are close to the Gospel in their style, in their simple, direct language, and especially in their contents. The path they trace out is certainly an arduous one, but it leads to the highest spiritual summits that can be reached in this life and promises us entrance into "the kingdom prepared . . . from the foundation of the world" (Mt 25:34). Even though some aspects of this spiritual journey can be daunting—for example, knowing and accepting that we are miserable wretches—we must acknowledge that the fundamental realities which the writings describe are profoundly true.

In his writings, Francis proposes many general rules of conduct based on the Gospel and human experience. None of these has become ineffectual or obsolete except, curiously enough, some of the more material and concrete demands which he made of his brothers and which are usually regarded as being central to his message. Some individual demands (such as poverty in dress and the use of money) and some collective demands (such as the refusal to own property in common) have long been seen as essential and special to the Franciscan Order. But for the Franciscans of today, they are only nostalgic memories, tinged with guilt, or a cause of reproach from others.

It is precisely on this point that we see how important it is to understand the message of Francis's writings as a whole and in the order of their importance. His vision of God and humanity, as well as the process of permanent conversion which he describes, will always be true and valid. These are the basic elements which we must accept and according to which we must regulate our lives. However, Francis showed that he was less literal and more evolutionary than is popularly supposed. In his attitude to material poverty, for example, he left us ample room for creative imagination, provided we do not strain out the gnat and swallow the camel.

Our whole study allows us to see how closely Francis's vision and its consequences for the Christian life follow the Gospel. It is a vision which is not confined to any one class of people. It challenges everyone equally and cannot be fully and finally realized either by an individual or by a community. Like the Church of Christ, it is a Utopia, not in the sense of something that is unreal or that cannot possibly exist, but as something towards which we try to advance day and night, towards which we stretch out our hands but never fully grasp here below.

When we see how far short we fall of the demands proposed by Francis, can we help feeling some remorse? And is this not more true when we measure ourselves against the standards of the Gospel of Christ to which Francis simply tried to call our attention and to which he could not and did not wish to add anything?

If our introduction to the message in Francis's writings causes the reader to ask these questions, it will have achieved its purpose.

The Task Remaining

In this study, we have examined methodically the vision conveyed by Francis's writings, his "message," but have not considered him as a historical figure or tried to interpret him as such. However, even though we have not been directly concerned with Francis in his actual historical context, we have always taken into account the profound influences which his contemporary surroundings had on him and, consequently, on his vision.

Still, I have, with some rare exceptions, deliberately refrained from appealing to the history of Francis which the biographical sources convey, as I have already explained in my introductory chapter. As we have seen (p. 17), G. Miccoli holds that Francis's writings should provide the criteria for evaluating these biographical sources and the interpretations they propose. This task, however, still remains to be carried out.

As a pioneer in this field, I have done my best to present the overall message which the writings contain explicitly or implicitly. My effort is a beginning which I hope others will continue by completing and correcting my work and, of course, contradicting me when necessary. This synthesis, such as it is, invites the reader to revise the image depicted in the innumerable hagiographic descriptions of Francis that have appeared, as well as those accounts of his spirituality that are centered on his personality.

While I do not deny the importance of this immense literature, I must honestly say that it misses the point. This large body of work starts from a number of historical data, which it immediately interprets in its own way. It then goes on to depict Francis as a "personality," a heroic figure, whose life and the words and deeds attributed to him then become his message. Consequently, the features of Francis's life which the literature singles out are the striking or surprising ones, which usually are external and are therefore only secondary to his message.

We believe that the essence of Francis's vision is to be found in his writings and in their order of importance. Therefore, researchers and those who study the literature on Francis, especially the older works, must examine it and its perspectives in the light of Francis's own vision.

This will not "destroy the icon" but will allow us to distinguish between the person and his message. It will free us from the stereotyped image of Francis as a poet, a revolutionary, or a radical ascetic. With its truth and realism, the message in his writings will show us what was in his heart and what he humbly proposes to us: God to be desired above all else, and our neighbor to be loved as a brother or sister.

Bibliography

[English translations are indicated when available.]

Writings of Francis:
Critical Editions and Global Analyses

Boehmer, H. *Analekten zur Geschichte des Franciscus von Assisi. S. Francisci opuscula, regula paenitentium, antiquissima de regula Minorum, de stigmatibus s. patris, de Sancto eiusque societate testimonia.* Tübingen et Leipzig, 1904.

Boehmer, H., F. Wiegand, et C. Andresen. *Analekten zur Geschichte des Franciscus von Assisi.* (3e éd.) Tübingen, 1961.

Claire et François d'Assise. *Écrits.* Introductions de Th. Matura. ("Foi vivante,"255). Paris, 1991.

Clare of Assisi: Early Documents. Trans. R. J. Armstrong, OFMCap. St. Bonaventure, NY: Franciscan Institute Publications, 1993.

Esser, K. *Die Opuscula des hl. Franziskus von Assisi. Neue textkritische Edition.* Rome, Grottaferrata, 1976.

—.*Opuscula Sancti Patris Francisci Assisiensis*; denuo edidit iuxta codices mss. Caietanus Esser. (2e éd.) Rome, Grottaferrata, 1978.

Francis and Clare: The Complete Works. Trans. Regis J. Armstrong OFMCap and Ignatius Brady OFM. Mahwah, NJ: Paulist Press, 1982.

François d'Assise. *Écrits.* Texte latin de l'édition K. Esser; introduction, traduction, notes, et index par Th. Desbonnets, J.-F. Godet, Th. Matura, et D. Vorreux (SC 285). Paris, 1981.

Godet J.-F. et G. Mailleux. *Opuscula sancti Francisci. Scripta sanctae Clarae.* Concordance, index, listes de fréquences, tables comparatives. (3e éd.) Louvain (CETEDOC), 1976.

Lemmens, L. *Opuscula sancti patris Francisci Assisiensis*, Quaracchi, 1904.

Paolazzi C. *Lettura degli"Scritti"di Francesco d'Assisi.* Milan, 1987.

Rodriguez Herrera, I. *Los escritos de San Francisco de Asis, traducción española y comentario filologico.* Murcie, 1985.

St. Francis of Assisi: Writings and Early Biography. English Omnibus of the Sources for the Life of St. Francis. Ed. Marion A. Habig. (4th ed.) Chicago: Franciscan Herald Press, 1983.

Collection of Thirteenth-Century Documents Relative to Francis.

Desbonnets, Th. et D. Vorreux. *Saint François d 'Assise. Documents. Écrits et premières biographies.* (2ᵉ éd.) Paris, 1981.

Books and Articles Used in Preparing this Work

Asseldonk, O. Van. *La lettera e lo spirito. Tensione vitale nel Francescanesimo ieri e oggi,* II. Rome, 1985.

—."Insegnamenti biblici 'privilegiati' negli scritti di San Francesco d'Assisi." Dans *ibid.,* 321-55. [English trans.: "Favored Biblical Teachings in the Writings of St. Francis of Assisi." *Greyfriars Review* 3:3 (1989): 287-314.]

—."Le lettere di San Pietro negli Scritti di S. Francesco." Dans *ibid.,* 429-41.

—."Lo Spirito del Signore e la sua santa operazione negli scritti di Francesco." Dans *ibid.,* 31-92. [English trans.: "The Spirit of the Lord and Its Holy Activity in the Writings of Francis." *Greyfriars Review* 5:1 (1991): 105-158.]

—."Maria, Sposa dello Spirito Santo." Dans *ibid.,* 125-35.

—."San Giovanni evangelista negli scritti di S. Francesco." Dans *ibid.,* 357-88.

—."*Sorores Minores.* Una nuova impostazione del problema." *Collectanea Franciscana* 62 (1992): 595-634.

—."Spirito Santo." Dans *La lettera . . . ,* 5-29.

Azzimonti, F. "Essai d'analyse théologique des écrits de saint François d'Assise." Lyon, 1970 (dact.).

Bartoli, Langeli A. "Gli Scritti da Francesco." Dans *Atti del XXI Convegno internazionale,* 101-59. Spolète, 1994.

Bartolini, R. *Lo spirito del Signore. Francesco di Assisi guida all'esperienza dello Spirito Sant.* Assise, 1982.

Brunette, P. *Essai d'analyse symbolique des "Admonitions" de François d'Assise.* Montréal, 1989.

Cardaropoli, G. et M. Conti. *Lettura biblico-teologica delle Fonti Francescane.* Rome, 1979.

Ciceri, A. "L'agire dell'uomo, l'uomo dell'azione. Una rilettura degli Opuscula S. Francisci, Assisiensis." Louvain-la-Neuve, 1994 (dact.).

Cominardi, J. C. *Quand la louange prend toute la place*. "Prier avec saint François." Paris, 1994.

Conti, M. *Studi e ricerche sul francescanesimo delle origini*. Rome, 1994.

Cornet, B. "Le *De reverentia Corporis Domini*, exhortation et lettre de S. François." *Études franciscaines* 6 (1955): 65-91, 167-80; 7 (1956): 20-35, 155-71; 8 (1957): 33-58.

Covi, E. et F. Raurell. *Metodi di lettura delle fonti francescane*. Rome, 1988.

Desbonnets, Th. "La Lettre à tous les fidèles de François d'Assise." Dans *I Frati Minori et il Terzo Ordine. Problemi e discussioni storiografich.e* Convegni del Centro di Studi sulla spiritualità medioevale, XXIII, 51-76. Todi, 1985.

—."*De l'intuition à l'institution. Les Franciscains*. Paris, 1983. [English trans.: *From Intuition to Institution: the Franciscans*. Chicago: Franciscan Herald Press, 1988.]

Dozzi, D. "Come Francesco cita e interpreta il Vangelo. Note metodologiche ed esemplificazioni." Dans Covi et Raurell, 176-98.

—."Tracee metodologiche in alcuni studiosi degli scritti di Francesco." Dans ibid., 28-51.

—.*Il Vangelo nella Regola non bollata di Francesco d 'Assisi*. Rome, 1989.

Dukker, Ch. *Umkehr des Herzens. Der Bussgedanke des hl. Franziskus von Assisi*. Werl, 1956.

Egger, W. *Nachfolge als Weg zum Leben. Chancen neuerer exegetischer Methoden dargelegt an Mk 10, 17-31*. Klosterneuburg, 1979.

Esser, K. *Anfänge und ursprüngliche Zielsetzungen des Ordens der Minderbrüder*. Leyde, 1966. [English trans.: *Origins of the Franciscan Order*. Trans. Aedan Daly and Irina Lynch. Chicago: Franciscan Herald Press, 1970.]

—."Die endgültige Regel der Minderen Brüder im Lichte der neuesten Forschung. Dans Grau, *Franziskanisches Leben. Gesammelte Dokumente*, 31-96. Werl, 1968.

—."Die *Regula pro eremitoriis data* des hl. Franziskus von Assisi." *Studien*: 137-179. [English trans.: "The *Regula Pro Emeritoriis Data* of St. Francis of Assisi," in *Franciscan Solitude*, 147-194. St. Bonaventure, NY: The Franciscan Institute, 1995.]

—.*Das Testament des hl. Franziskus von Assisi. Eine Untersuchung über seine Echtheit und seine Bedeutung*. Münster, 1949.

—."La lettera di San Francesco ai fedeli." *L 'Ordine della Penitenza di San Francesco d'Assisi nel secolo XIII*, 65-78. Rome, 1973.

—.*Le Ammonizioni di San Francesco*. (4ᵉ éd.) Rome, 1982. [English trans.: "Meditations on the *Admonitions* of St. Francis of Assisi." *Greyfriars Review* 6:Supplement (1992): 1-174.]

—.*Studien zu den Opuscula des hl. Franziskus von Assisi*. Rome, 1972.

—.*Thèmes spirituels*. Paris, 1958. [English trans.: *Repair My House*. Trans. Michael D. Meilach. Chicago: Franciscan Herald Press, 1963.]

—."Über die Chronologie der Schriften des Hl. Franziskus." *Studien*, 299-340.

Esser, K. et E. Grau. *Antwort der Liebe. Der Weg des franziskanischen Menschen zu Gott*. Werl, 1958; trad. fse: *La Conversion du cœur* et *Pour le Royaume*. Paris, 1960. [English trans.: *Love's Reply*. Trans. Ignatius Brady. Chicago: Franciscan Herald Press, 1963.]

Flood, D. *Die"Regula non bullata"der Minderbrüder*. Werl, 1967.

—.*Frère François et le mouvement franciscain*. Paris, 1983.

—.*Francis of Assisi and the Franciscan Movement*. Quezon City, 1989.

Flood, D., W. Van Dijk, et Th. Matura. *La Naissance d'un charisme. Une lecture de la première règle de François d'Assise*. Paris, 1973. [English trans.: *The Birth of a Movement: a Study of the First Rule of St. Francis*. Trans. Paul Schwartz and Paul Lachance. Chicago: Franciscan Herald Press, 1975.]

Freyer, I. B. *Der demütige und geduldige Gott. Franziskus und sein Gottesbild-ein Vergleich mit der Tradition*. Rome, 1989.

Gallant, L. "*Dominus regnavit a ligno. L'Officium Passionis* de saint François d'Assise. Édition critique et étude." Thèse manuscrite. Institut catholique de Paris, 1978.

—."L'Évangéliaire de S. François d'Assise." *Collectanea Franciscana*, 53 (1983), 5-22; 54 (1984), 241-60.

Galot, J. "La Relation de Marie avec l'Esprit Saint." *Esprit et vie*, 99 (1989), 440-47.

Gniecki, C. *Visione dell'uomo negli Scritti di Francesco d'Assisi*. Rome, 1987.

Holter, B. "*Zum besonderen Dienst bestellt*": *Die Sicht des Priesteramtes bei Franz von Assisi*. Werl, 1992.

Ilarino da Milano. *La spiritualità evangelica nei secoli XIᵉ-XIIᵉ*. Rome, 1971.

Koper, R. *Das Weltverständnis des hl. Franziskus von Assisi. Eine Untersuchung über das "Exivi de saeculo."* Werl, 1959.

Lanne, E. "The Life of St. Antony by St. Athanasius the Great." *Proche-Orient chrétien*, 42 (1992): 243-59.

Lapsanski, D. V. *Perfectio evangelica*. Munich, 1974. [English trans.: *Evangelical Perfection: an Historical Examination of the Concept in the Early Franciscan Sources*. St. Bonaventure, N.Y.: The Franciscan Institute, 1977.]

Lauriola, G. *Introduzione a Francesco d'Assisi*. Noci, 1986.

Leclerc, E. *Le Cantique des créatures, ou les Symboles de l'union*. Paris, 1970. [English trans.: *The Canticle of Creatures: Symbols of Union: an Analysis of St. Francis of Assisi*. Trans. Matthew J. O'Connell. Chicago: Franciscan Herald Press, 1976.]

—.*Un maître à prier: François d'Assise*. Paris, 1993.

—.*La Sagesse d'un pauvre*. (15ᵉ éd.) Paris, 1991. [English trans.: *Wisdom of The Poverello*. Trans. Marie Louise Johnson. Chicago: Franciscan Herald Press, 1961.]

Lehmann, L. "*Gratias agimus tibi*. Structure and Content of Chapter XXIII of the *Regula non bullata*." *Laurentianum*, 23 (1982): 312-75. [English trans.: "'We Thank You.' The Structure and Content of Chapter 23 of the *Earlier Rule*." *Greyfriars Review* 5:1 (1991): 1-54.]

—.*Franziskus Meister des Gebets*. Werl, 1989.

—.*Tiefe und Weite. Der universale Grundzug in den Gebeten des Franziskus von Assisi*. Werl, 1984.

Manns, F. "François d'Assise. Exégète. Introduction: vrai ou faux problème?" Dans *Francesco d'Assisi, nel 750ᵐᵒ della morte* (1226-1976). Jérusalem, 1976

Matura, Th. "'Le cœur tourné vers le Seigneur.' La dimension contemplative de la vie chrétienne d'après les écrits de François." *La Vie des commaunutés religieuses*, 51 (1993): 259-73.

—."Comment François lit et interprète l'Évangile." *Évangile aujourd'hui*, 88 (1975): 55-63.

—."*Dieu le Père très saint*"contemplé par François. Paris, 1990.

—."L'Église dans les écrits de François." *Antonianum*, 57 (1982): 94-112.

—."Évangélisation ou accueil de l'Évangile par François et ses frères." *La Vie des communautés religieuses*, 51 (1993): 3-24.

—."Le prospettive teologiche e spirituali nelle preghiere di S. Francesco." *Quaderni di Spiritualità Francescana, Quaderno IX*. La Verna, 1986.

—."*Mi Pater sancte*. Dieu comme Père dans les écrits de François." *Laurentianum*, 23 (1982): 102-32. [English trans.: "'My Holy Father!' God as Father in the Writings of St. Francis." *Greyfriars Review* 1:1 (1987): 105.]

—."Les Noms divins." Dans *Dieu le Père très saint* . . . , 123-34.

—.*Prier quinze jours avec François d'Assise*. Paris, 1994.

—.*Le Projet évangélique de François d'Assise aujourd'hui*. Paris, 1977. [English trans.: *The Gospel Life of Francis of Assisi Today*. Trans. Paul Lachance and Paul Schwartz. Chicago: Franciscan Herald Press, 1980.]

—."Sequela Christi." *Dizionario Francescano*. (2ᵉ éd.) Padoue, 1995.

—."Vision qui se dégage des écrits de François." *François d'Assise, Écrits* (SC 285), 49-81.

Meersseman, G. G. *Dossier de l'ordre de la Pénitence au XIIIᵉ siècle*. Fribourg, 1961.

Menesto, E. "Gli scritti di Francesco d'Assisi." Dans *Atti del XXI convegno internazionale*, 161-181. Spolète, 1994.

Miccoli, G. "La proposta cristiana di Francesco d'Assisi." *Francesco d'Assisi*, 33-97. Turin, 1991. [English trans.: "Francis of Assisi's Christian Proposal." *Greyfriars Review* 3:2 (1989): 127-172.]

—."Un' esperienza cristiana tra Vangelo e istituzione." Dans *Atti del XVIII convegno internazionale*, 5-40. Spolète, 1992.

—."Tavola rotonda." Dans *ibid.*, (1994), 253-59; 284-88.

Nguyen-Van-Khanh, N. *Le Christ dans la pensée de saint François d'Assise d'après ses écrits*. Paris, 1989.

Pellegrini, L. "Francesco e i suoi scritti. Problemi e orientamenti di lettura in alcuni recenti studi." *Rivista di Storia della Chiesa in Italia*, 36 (1982), 311-31.

—."Un secolo di 'lettura' delle fonti biografiche di Francesco d'Assisi." Dans Covi et Raurell, 52-79. [English trans.: "A Century Reading the Sources for the Life of St. Francis of Assisi." *Greyfriars Review* 7:3 (1993): 323-346.]

Raurell, F. "La lettura del *Cantico dei Cantici* al tempo di Chiara et la *IV Lettera ad Agnese di Praga*." *Laurentianum*, 31 (1990): 198-309.

Rotzetter, A. *Die Funktion der franziskanischen Bewegung in der Kirche. Eine pastoraltheologische Interpretation der grundlegenden franziskanischen Texte*. Schwyz, 1977.

—."Franziskusdeutung als Forschung und Vermittlung." Dans Covi et Raurell, 116-42.

Sabatier, P. *Vie de saint François d'Assise.* Paris, 1894. [English trans.: *Life of St. Francis of Assisi.* Trans. Louise Seymour Houghton. New York: C. Scribner's Sons, 1894.]

—."Examen de quelques travaux récents sur les opuscules de saint François." *Opuscules de critique historique* 10 (1904): 1-48.

Schampheleer, J. de. *L'Office de la Pâque. Commentaire de l' "Officium Passionis" de S. François d 'Assise.* Paris, 1963.

Schmucki, O. "Gli scritti legislativi di san Francesco." Dans Cardaropoli et Conti, *Approccio storicocritico*, 73-98.

—."*Ignorans sum et idiota.* Das Ausmass der schulischen Bildung des hl. Franziskus von Assisi." *Studia historico-ecclesiastica. Festgabe für Prof. Luchesius G. Spätling*, 283-310. Rome, 1977. [English trans.: "St. Francis's Level of Education." *Greyfriars Review* 10:2 (1996): 153-17.]

—."La 'forma di vita secondo il Vangelo' gradatamente scoperta da S. Francesco d'Assisi." *Italia Francescana*, 59 (1984): 341-405. [English trans.: "The Way of Life According to the Gospel as It Was Discovered by St. Francis of Assisi." *Greyfriars Review* 2:3 (1988): 1-56.]

—."La *Lettera a tutto l'Ordine* di San Francesco." *Italia Francescana*, 55 (1980): 245-85. [English trans.: "St. Francis's *Letter to the Entire Order.*" *Greyfriars Review* 3:1 (1989): 1-33.]

—."Linee fondamentali della *Forma vitae* nell'esperienza di san Francesco." Dans Cardaropoli et Conti, *Lettura biblico-teologica*, 183-231. [English trans.: "Fundamental Characteristics of the Franciscan 'Form of Life.'" *Greyfriars Review* 5:3 (1991): 325-366.]

—."Zur Mystik des hl. Franziskus von Assisi im Lichte seiner Schriften." Dans *Abendländische Mystik im Mittelalter*, 241-68. Stuttgart, 1986. [English trans.: "Mysticism of St. Francis in the Light of His Writings." *Greyfriars Review* 3:3 (1989): 241-266.]

Scivoletto, N. "Problemi di lingua e di stile degli scritti latini di S. Francesco." Dans *Atti del IV convegno internazionale*, 103-124. Assise, 1977.

Spirito, G. A. *El cielo en la tierra. La inhabitación trinitaria en San Francisco a la luz de su tiempo y de sus escritos.* Rome, 1994.

Spiteris, G. "Francesco d'Assisi profeta dell' incontro tra Occidente e Oriente." *Laurentianum*, 26 (1985): 453-493.

Stanislao da Campagnola. *L'angelo del sesto sigillo e l' "alter Christus." Genesi e sviluppo di due temi francescani nei secoli XIII-XIV.* Rome, 1971.

—.*Le origini francescane come problema storiografico*. (2ᵉ éd.) Pérouse, 1979

Vaiani, C. *La via di Francesco. Una sintesi della spiritualità francescana partire dagli scritti di san Francesco*. Milan, 1993.

Vandenbroucke, F. "Printemps franciscain." Dans *Histoire de la spiritualité chrétienne*, t. II, 345-381. Paris, 1961. [English trans.: "The Franciscan Spring." In *The Spirituality of the Middle Ages*, 283-314. Vol. 2 of *A History of Christian Spirituality*. New York: The Seabury Press, 1968.]

Verhey, A. *Der Mensch unter der Herrschaft Gottes. Versuch einer Theologie des Menschen nach dem hl. Franziskus von Assisi*. Düsseldorf, 1960.

Viviani, W. *L'ermeneutica di Francesco d'Assisi. Indagine alla luce di Gv 13-17 nei suoi scritti*. Rome, 1983.

Vollot, B. "La *Première Règle* de saint François et l'harmonie évangélique." *Foi et langage*, 6 (1982): 89-102 ; 181-91; 276-86.

—."Le *Diatessaron* et la *Première Règle* de saint François." *Franziskanische Studien*, 72 (1990), 341-64. [English trans.: "The *Diatessaron* and the *Earlier Rule* of St. Francis." *Greyfriars Review* 6:3 (1992): 279-317.]

—."Césaire de Spire et la règle de 1221." *Laurentianum*, 32 (1991), 3-28; 173-220.

Zweerman, Th. *"Timor Domini*. Versuch einer Deutung der 27 Ermahnung des hl. Franziskus von Assisi." *Franziskanische Studien*, 60 (1978): 202-23.